MIND PATTERNS FOR COMPETITIVE EXAMS

JEE,NEET,UPSC,CAT,CUET.NDA,NTSE,KVPY

ACHARYA VISHVENDRA

Made with ♥ on the Notion Press Platform
www.notionpress.com

DEDICATED TO THE EMOTIONAL CONFLICTS I FELT DURING MY PREPARATION OF JEE.

Contents

Foreword

Normally students have under-developed **"MIND-BRAIN SYSTEM",**As an impact of which they have poor **information processing skills.**There is a pattern to develop the **"MIND-BRAIN SYSTEM".**

In this book we have tried to explore a **"MIND TRAINING PROGRAM"** for learning the **PATTERNS** of the **"MIND-BRAIN SYSTEM"** so that they can have **information processing skills** compatible with the competitive exams.

Preface

Preparing for competitive exams is a very challenging task.its not so simple that you just study and can crack competitive exam.There are hidden dimensions which are normally not known to the people.

if we analyse the successful students in competitive exams we can find that only those students are able to crack competitive exams whose parents started working on them since class 5 or earlier,thsy started gradually wrking on the"**MIND-BRAIN SYSTEM**" of the student by following an **information processing model.**

Normally students **don't like** to study.They want to **avoid study**,because normally they just want to react to the **present events**.Studies involves access to **hidden dimensions** and first reaction of the **brain** is a state of **flight mode activation**.students will find **excuse** to run away from the uncomfortable feelings during **studies**.

but if we **can train** students to learn gradually how to deal with emotional conflicts with a strong will power then gradually students can learn how to deal with the emotional conflicts during studies and can develop a system of **information processing** and can crack **competitive exams** successfully.

This book is about the training to develop the system of **information processing** within a student so that he can actually prepare for **competitive exam** rather than **acting to prepare**.

Acknowledgements

Thanks to the situations of life which stimulated me to work on the fundamental concept of **effective learning** via **effective information processing skills,**

Prologue

The universe is being guided by **hidden rules**,just decode **the rules** and get what you **deserve.**

If you aspire **your child** to be successful in **cracking a competitve exam** then its **not sufficient** to just enroll him in an **education system**,you have to pay him **personal attention** and check his **progress** yourself.

Check yourself about the **"INFORMATION PROCESSING SKILLS"** of your child.Just ask him what he has **studied today** and observe his reactions **silently**.observe his **face reactions** and see yourself that is he really able to **process the information** or just gets **afraid,nervous,worried,anxious**,or make **false stories.**

if your child is having these **symptoms** then you need to follow a **system** to make him aware that making **false stories** may be **ok to deal with daily life** but when it is concerned with the skills for your career then making **false stories** are of **no use** because in your career,nobody cares about **what you say**,they just care about **what you do.**

this book is an effort to **develop a mechanism** for learning the **MIND-BRAIN PATTERNS** for **competiitve exams**

CHAPTER ONE

INTRODUCTION

1.1:COMPETITIVE EXAMS:

competitive exams are held in our country every year to ensure that only brightest young minds are able to reach the top colleges or positions and can lead the country to achieve the goal of a developed nation.but selection rate in these exams are very low.For ex: in **JEE/NEET** only about 1.7 percent students are able to get admissions,the same thing is applicable to other eaxms like: **CUET,UPSC,GATE,NDA,NTSE,KVPY etc.**

So one thing is very clear that these are **screening exams** which are based on **psycologically designed patterns** to test the "**MIND-BRAIN SYSTEMS**",hence t**o crack these exams** focus should be on **learning the patterns of these competitive exams.**

FIG-1.1:COMPETITIVE EXAMS IN INDIA

1.2:PATTERNS IN COMPETITIVE EXAMS:

Competitive exams are about solving questions or problems.when we solve a question our "MIND-BRAIN SYSTEM"folllows a certain pattern for example:

Lets start by solving a simple question.

How many seconds are there in a minute?

Most of us can immidiately retain the answer as 60 seconds

Now focus on the process which your "**MIND-BRAIN SYSTEM**" followed to find this answer.You must have felt that there is some information processing system within you which just gave you answer.

now lets make this question a bit complex

How many seconds are there in an hour?

this question is a bit harder than the first.now i hope most of the people will use an algorithm and will try to connect the relation between seconds,minutes and hours.most of people have used the pattern like 1 minute=60 seconds,1 hour=60 minutes and hence 1 hour=60 minute=60*60 seconds=3600 seconds

Similarly there is a pattern in solving problems asked in competitive exams.those who learn this pattern are able to crack competitive exams with flying colours whereas those who are not compatible with decoding the pattern just struggle with information,thoughts,emotions/energy & finally end up as a non productive human resource.

so learning the mind patterns for competitive exams is needed for optimal success in competitive exams.

hence we introduce a training program of 21 days for learning the mentral patterns for competitive exams so that students can actually prepare for competitive exams rather than just acting to prepare.

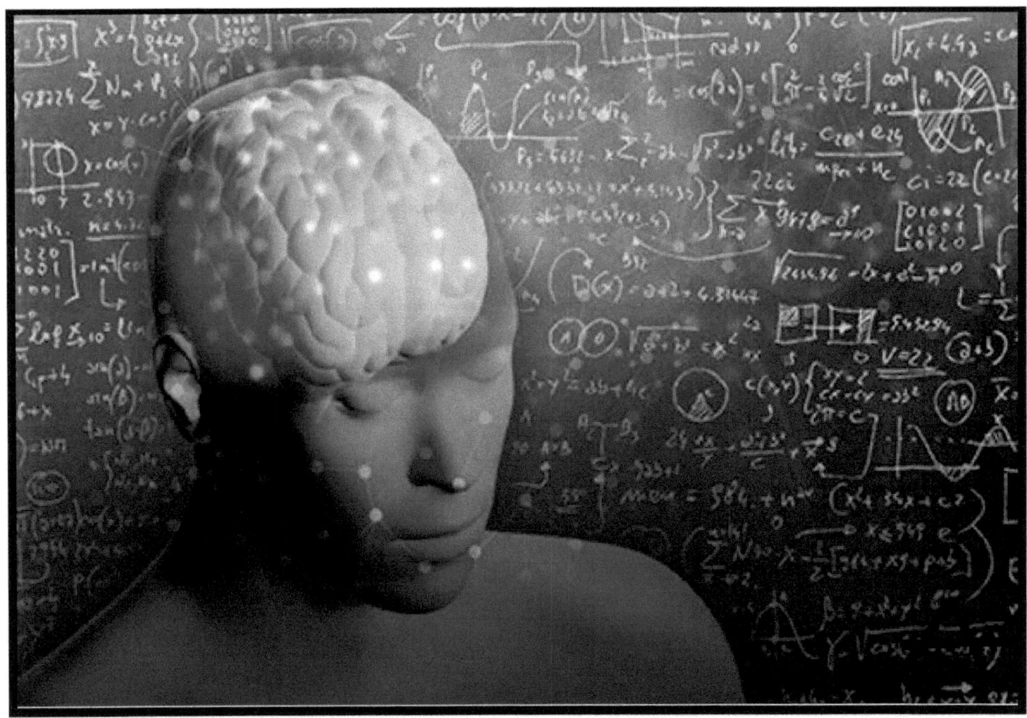

FIG-1.2:USE OF "MIND PATTERNS" FOR SOLVING A QUESTION

1.3:OUR "MIND-BRAIN SYSTEM":

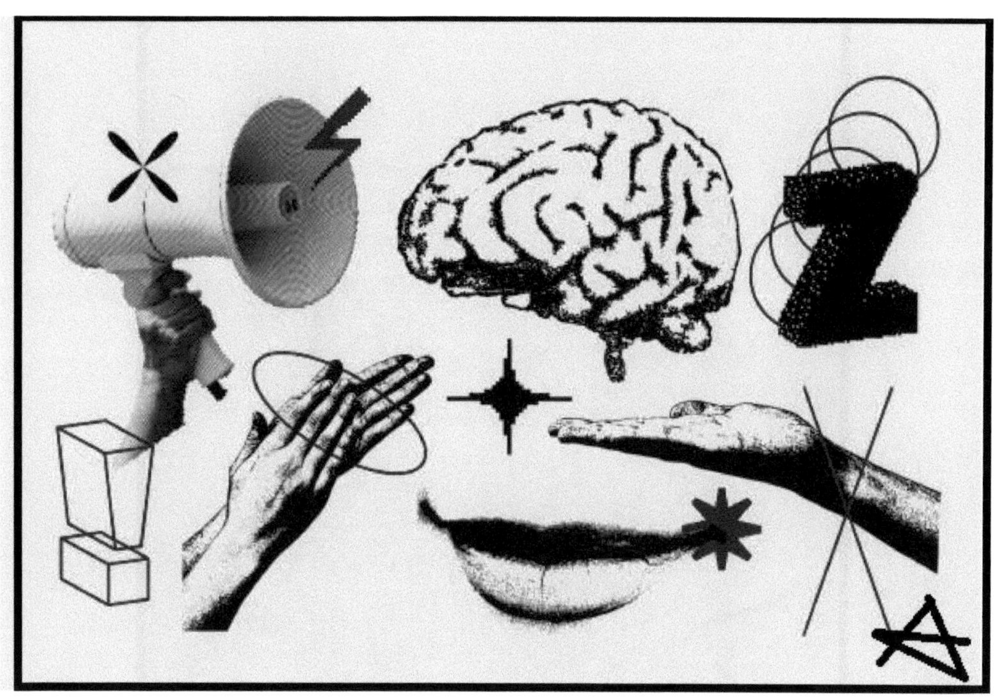

FIG-1.3: OUR MIND-BRAIN SYSTEM

Our **"MIND-BRAIN SYSTEM"** receives & process information from our 5 senses by following a pattern.Similarly when a student prepare for competitive exams his **"MIND-BRAIN SYSTEM"** follows a certain pattern.

FIG-1.4:USE OF MENTAL PATTERN BY A HUMAN BEING TO MAP INFORMATION

1.4: HUMAN "BRAIN":

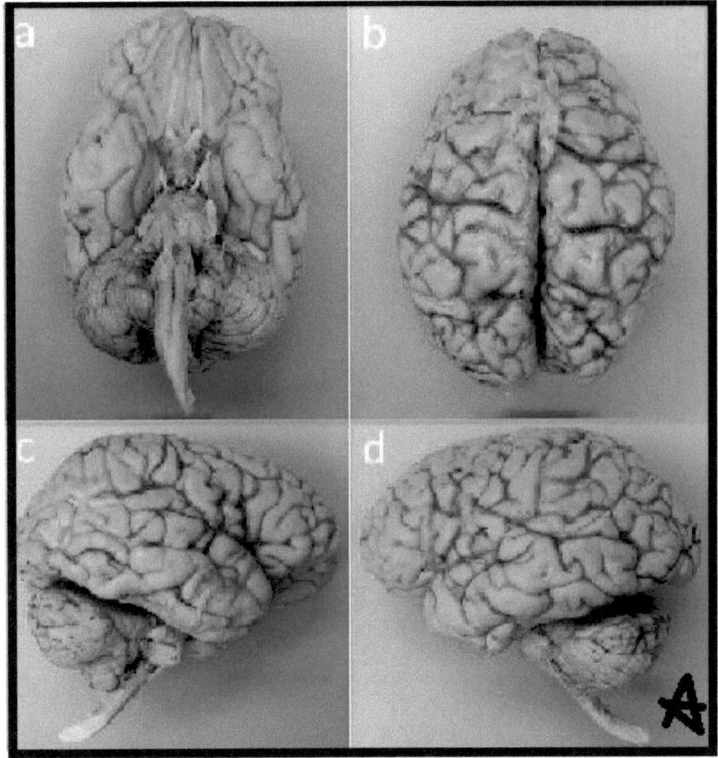

FIG-1.5: HUMAN BRAIN

The human brain is made up of many specialized areas that work together:

- The cortex is the outermost layer of brain cells. Thinking and voluntary movements begin in the cortex.
- The brain stem is between the spinal cord and the rest of the brain. Basic functions like breathing and sleep are controlled here.
- The basal ganglia are a cluster of structures in the center of the brain. The basal ganglia coordinate messages between multiple other brain areas.
- The cerebellum is at the base and the back of the brain. The cerebellum is responsible for coordination and balance.

The brain is also divided into several lobes:

- The frontal lobes are responsible for problem solving and judgment and motor function.
- The parietal lobes manage sensation, handwriting, and body position.
- The temporal lobes are involved with memory and hearing.
- The occipital lobes contain the brain's visual processing system.

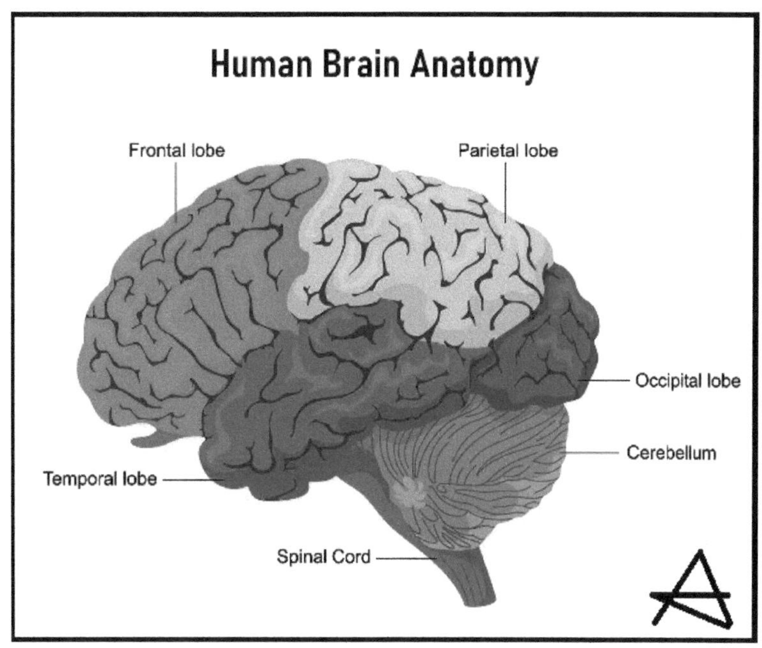

FIG-1.6: HUMAN BRAIN ANATOMY

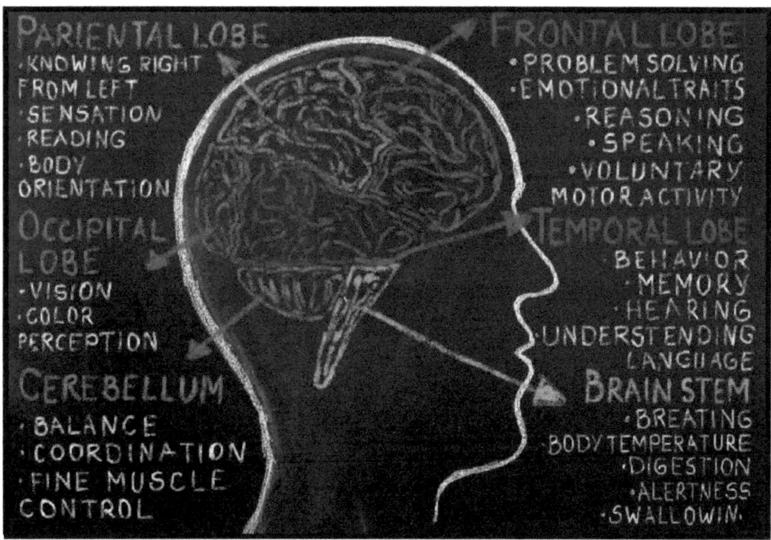

FIG-1.7:DIFFERENT PARTS OF THE BRAIN

1.4:HUMAN MIND:

As per sigmund freuds pschoanalytical theory,human mind can be explained in terms of an iceberg comprising of:

1.The conscious mind

2.The pre-conscious/sub conscious mind

3.The unconscious mind

FIG-1.8: HUMAN MIND

In 1923, Freud created the model of the mind that is still used today. He detailed the unconscious, preconscious, and conscious mind while also developing a theory involving the id, ego, and superego.

Unconscious Mind:

The unconscious mind holds thoughts and feelings that we cannot easily access. In other words, unconscious thoughts and desires are what drive our behavior.

This part of the mind also holds undesirable drives, instincts, repressed traumas, and painful emotions. In a way, it prevents these things from entering the conscious mind.

Think of it as a storage container for all thoughts, memories, and knowledge that is no longer of use.

Preconscious Mind

The preconscious, also known as the subconscious, is where our long-term memories are stored. It holds all the mental processes that we are not currently aware of but can easily be brought back to consciousness.

Conscious Mind

The conscious is where our current thoughts and feelings reside. It is everything you are aware of and correlates to short-term memory. This part of the mind also controls logical and critical thinking.

1.5:THE MIND MAPPING:

Take a deep breath and just try to think what you have done today.you can retain most of the events that happened with you precisely,so there is some memory card inside us which is recording everything happening with us.we can't manipulate this recorder even if we wish to.

so we can say that there is a natural information recorder within us which maps information from the conscious to unconscious mind.now here is the key.

there is a pattern to connect the conscious and unconscious mind.Those students who know this pattern are able to solve questions in their exam.whereas those students who don't know this pattern are unable to retrieve information from their unconscious mind and are unable to solve questions in their exam.

hence the entire turning point in the preparation of competitive exams is the **patterns of connecting the conscious and unconscious mind.**

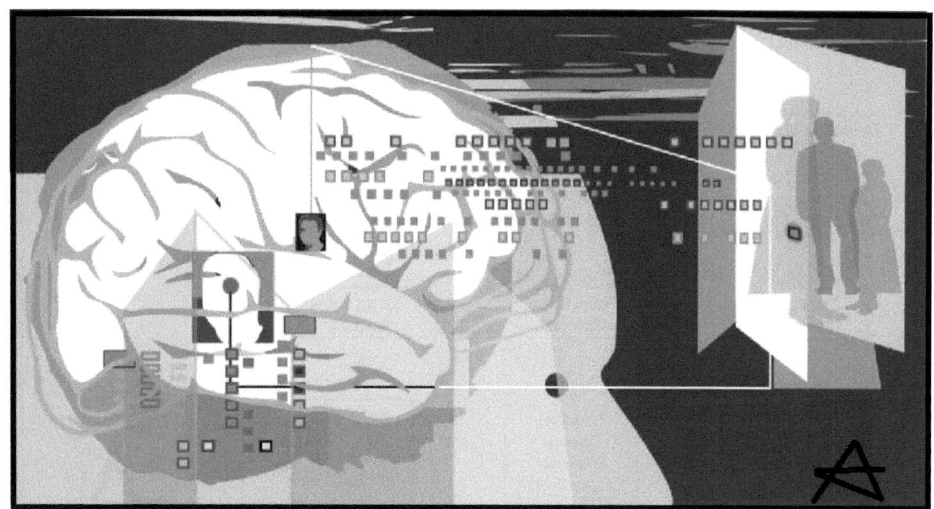

FIG-1.9:MIND PATTERNS OF CONNECTING CONSCIOUS & UNCONSCIOUS MIND

1.6:INFORMATION PROCESSING THEORY:

Atkinson and Shiffrin's stage theory:

This theory was introduced by atkinson and shiffrin & later modified by other researchers but the basic outline of stage theory continues to be a cornerstone of information processing theory. The model concerns how information is stored in memory and presents a sequence of three stages, as follows:

Sensory Memory — Sensory memory involves whatever we take in through our senses. This kind of memory is exceedingly brief, only lasting up to 3 seconds. In order for something to enter sensory memory, the individual has to pay attention to it. Sensory memory can't attend to every piece of information in the environment, so it filters out what it deems irrelevant and only sends what seems important to the next stage, short-term memory. The information that's most likely to reach the next stage is either interesting or familiar.

Short-Term Memory/Working Memory — Once information reaches short-term memory, which is also called working memory, it is filtered further. Once again, this kind of memory doesn't last long, only about 15 to 20 seconds. However, if information is repeated, which is referred to as maintenance rehearsal, it can be stored for up to 20 minutes. As observed by Miller, working memory's capacity is limited so it can only process a certain number of pieces of information at a time. How many pieces is not agreed on, although many still point to Miller to identify the number as five to nine.

There are several factors that will impact what and how much information will be processed in working memory. Cognitive load capacity varies from person to person and from moment to moment based on an individual's cognitive abilities, the amount of information being processed, and one's ability to focus and pay attention. Also, information that is familiar and has often been repeated doesn't require as much cognitive capacity and, therefore, will be easier to process. For example, riding a bike or driving a car take minimal cognitive load if you've performed these tasks numerous times. Finally, people will pay more attention to information they believe is important, so that information is more likely to be processed. For example, if a student is preparing for a test, they are more likely to attend to information that will be on the test and forget about information they don't believe they will be asked about.

Long-Term Memory — Although short-term memory has a limited capacity, the capacity of long-term memory is thought to be limitless. Several different types of information are encoded and organized in long-term memory: declarative information, which is information that can be discussed such as facts, concepts, and ideas (semantic memory) and personal experiences (episodic memory); procedural information, which is information about how to do something like drive a car or brush your teeth; and imagery, which are mental pictures.

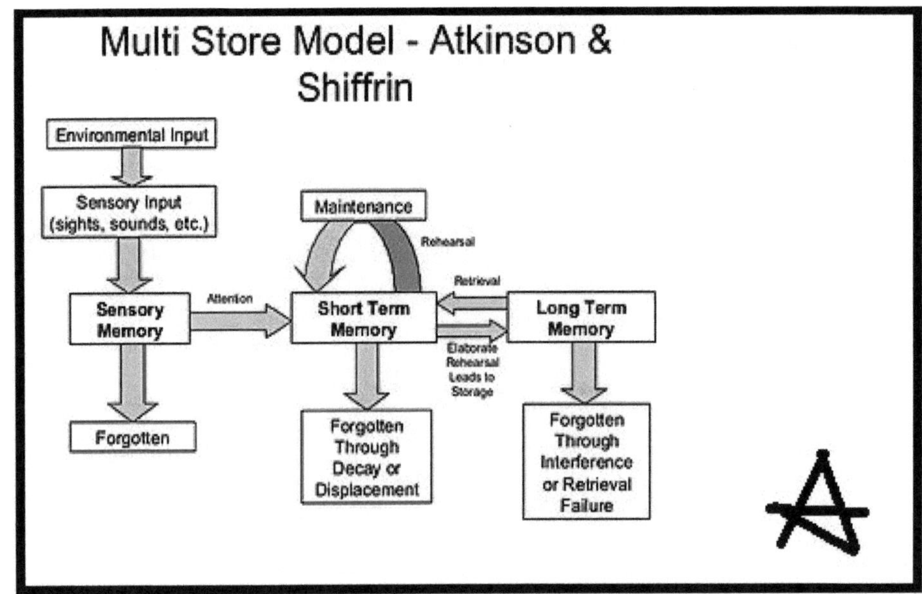

FIG-1.10: ATKINSON & SHIFFRIN MODEL

Hence we can say that our mind uses a pattern to process the information as predicted by the information processing theory.Those students who are able to process information effectively performs better than other students.

These students actually learn through active learning rather than passive learning in which they engage and participate in learning rather than just writing information.

lets discuss about active learning in the next chapter.

CHAPTER TWO

ACTIVE LEARNING STATE

2.1:NORMAL MIND STATE:

Normally a student is mentally in a passive learning state.He is trapped in imaginations,thoughts or some kind of unrealistic state of mind.As an impact of which he is not able to learn effectively and retrieve effectively during exams.

FIG-1.11: A NORMAL STUDENT IN PASSIVE LEARNING STATE

To learn effectively its necessary to change the state of mind.or more specifically the brainwave frequencies.For effective learning and problem solving we need to modulate the brainwave frequencies from theta to beta.

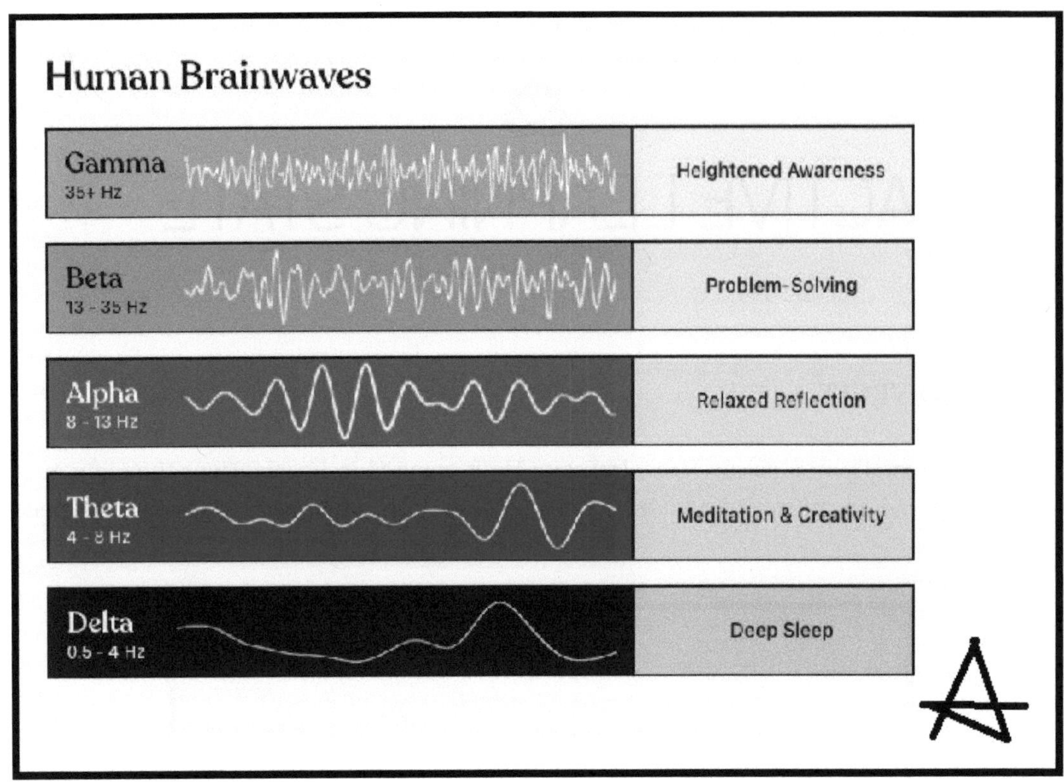

FIG-1.12: INCREASE BRAINWAVE FREQUENCIES FOR EFFECTIVE LEARNING

2.2:ACTIVE LEARNING METHODS:

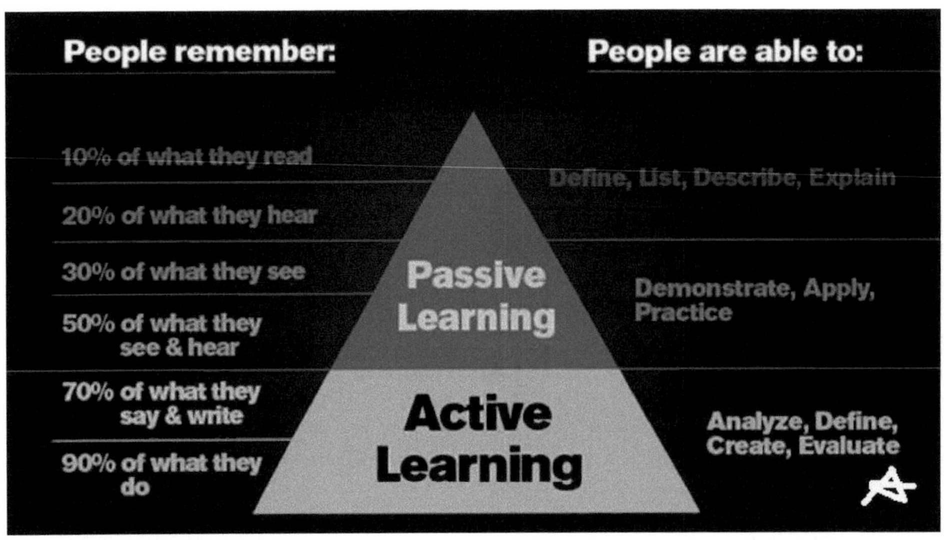

FIG-1.13: ACTIVE LEARNING

These methods allow students to engage in their learning by being involved in learning as a spontaneous process and thinking, discussing, investigating, and creating.

students practice the real process of learning and develop skills, design problems solutions, deal with complex problems and their solutions,

Analysing the learning process is critical to active learning process. Education research shows that incorporating active learning methods into classrooms sunstantially improves the outcomes.

hence we can conclude that the methods of active learning involves:

1.Focus on present rather than past or future
2.Think,analyse,develop models
3.Evaluation or feedback of output

2.3:Benefits of active learning:

Active learning increases productivity and enables a student to develop himself as an effective human resource

1.It stimulates the gradual development of real world problem-solving skills
2.it stimulates students to develop their integrated information processing skills
3. It explores the path of developing self confidence in Students
4.It stimulates students to learn how to take risks and build self-confidence
5.It stimulates students for developing creative thinking skills
6. it guides students to undergo customized learning as per their capabilities

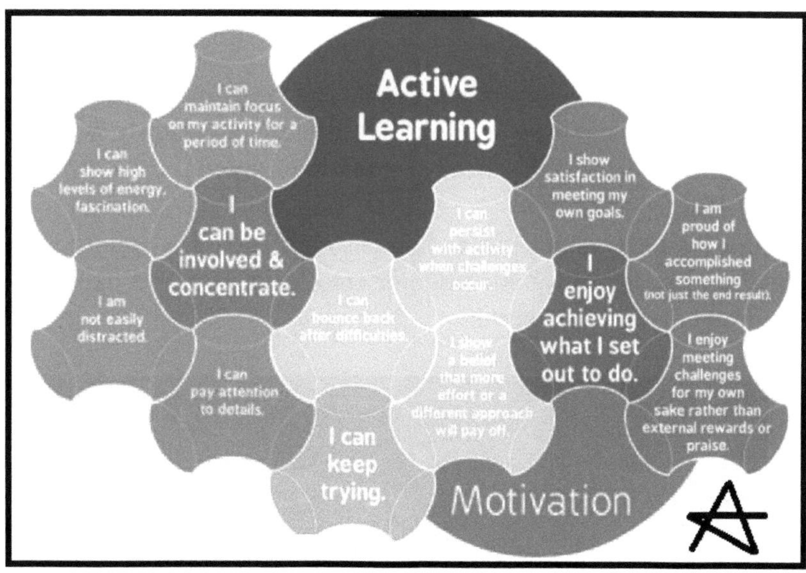

FIG-1.14: BENIFITS OF ACTIVE LEARNING

2.4:HOW TO START ACTIVE LEARNING :

As explained earlier normally a student is in monkey mind or unstable mind state.He is reacting to the different thoughts and emotions present in his "**MIND-BRAIN SYSTEM**",In this state of mind a student **can't learn anything** as he will keep switching between **different thoughts and emotions.**

so the first step in active learning is switching the unstable thought pattern to stable thought pattern.For this students must focus on present and increase their brainwave frequency when the brainwave frequency has switched to beta then thought patterns switches from unstable to stable and students can be further trained for active learning.

so the various steps in active learning may be as:

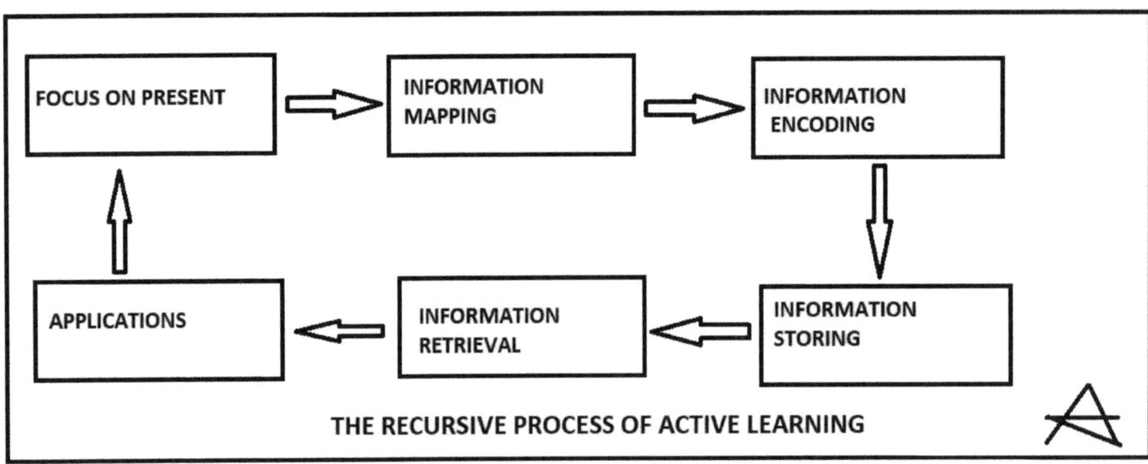

FIG-1.15: STEPS OF ACTIVE LEARNING

1.FOCUSING ON PRESENT:

Start with a simple exercise to focus on present.try to focus first on your right ear then on left year.similarly first see through your right eye then through left eye.this technique is basically focusing you on sensory memory which is the first layer of our "**MIND-BRAIN SYSTEM**".

2.INFORMATION MAPPING:

After focusing the next task is to map the new information with the information already present in our "**MIND-BRAIN SYSTEM**".Its a challenging task and must be processed **carefully and slowly** so that

You are able to map new information with the already present information.

3.INFORMATION ENCODING:

After information mapping the next task is information encoding.there is a pattern to encode new information into another format consisting of some sort of attraction or emotions,which acts like glue to connect information received from our external world to our inner world.

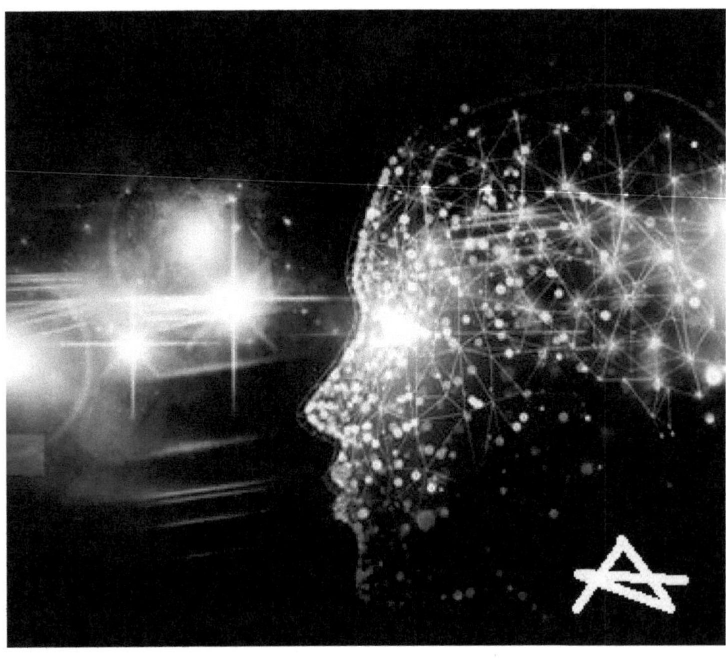

FIG-1.16: INFORMATION ENCODING

4.INFORMATION STORING:

The next task is storing information in your mind.Information storing is a crucial step as it forms the basis of information processing which is the foundation purpose of our own existence.

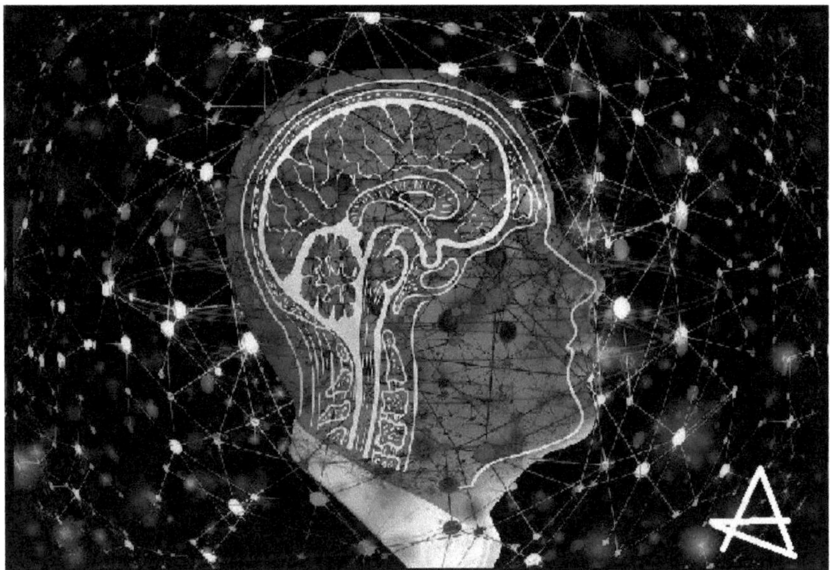

FIG-1.17: INFORMATION STORING

5.INFORMATION RETRIEVAL:

information retrieval refers to the process of retrieving information as and when needed.For example:'when a student appears for a test,he need to retrieve the entire information which he/she has learnt during last 1 or 2 years.hence information retrieval is the key factor to decide a better mind brain system from rest of others.

FIG-1.18: INFORMATION RETRIEVAL

CHAPTER THREE

INFORMATION PROCESSING MODEL

3.1:MULTI STORE MODEL & WORKING MEMORY MODEL:

There are various attempts to develop models of information processing. The two most popular are the multi-store model by **Atkinson and Shiffrin** and the **working memory model by Baddeley and Hitch.**

3.2:Atkinson and Shiffrin Model:

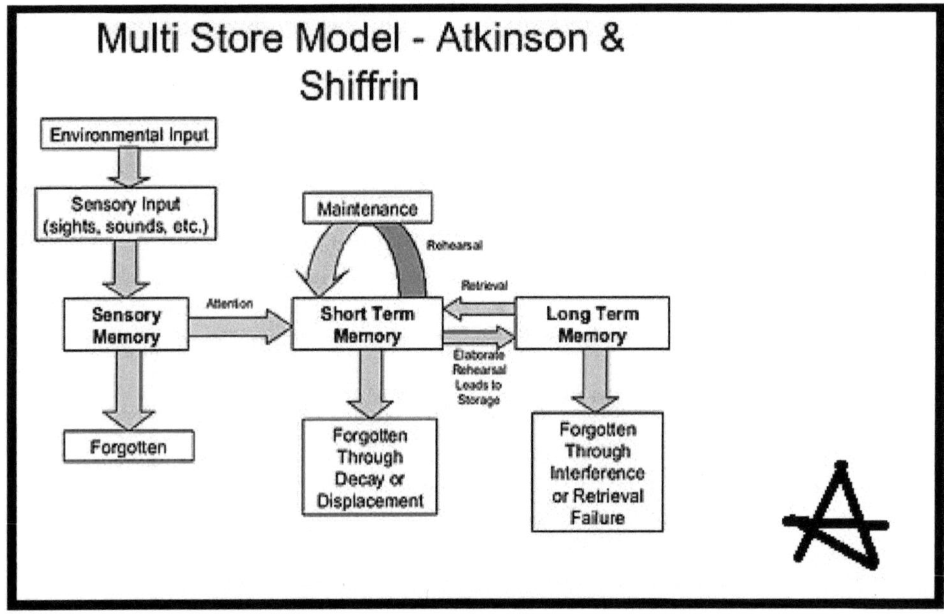

FIG-1.19:ATKINSON'S & SHIFFRIN MODEL

John William Atkinson and Richard Shiffrin proposed the multi-store model in 1968 to illustrate their view of human memory (Atkinson & Shiffrin, 1977). The model shows the three subsections of human memory and how they work together.

So, what are the 3 stages of information processing? They are as follows:

Sensory Memory – It holds the information that the mind perceives through various senses such as visual, olfactory, or auditory information. These sense organs often receive a barrage of stimuli all the time. However, most are ignored and forgotten by the mind to prevent getting overwhelmed. When sensory information engages and gets the attention of the mind, it is transferred to short-term memory.

Short-Term Memory (Working Memory) – Information in short-term memory only lasts around 30 seconds. Cognitive abilities affect how individuals process information in working memory. Additionally, attention and focus on the most important information also play an important role in encoding it into long-term memory. Furthermore, repetition significantly helps the ability to remember details for a long time.

Long-Term Memory – It is thought that long-term memory has an unlimited amount of space as it can store memories from a long time ago to be retrieved at a later time. Various methods are used to store information in the long-term memory such as repetition, connecting information, relating information to meaningful experience or other information, and breaking up the information into smaller chunks.

3.3:Baddeley and Hitch Model of Working Memory:

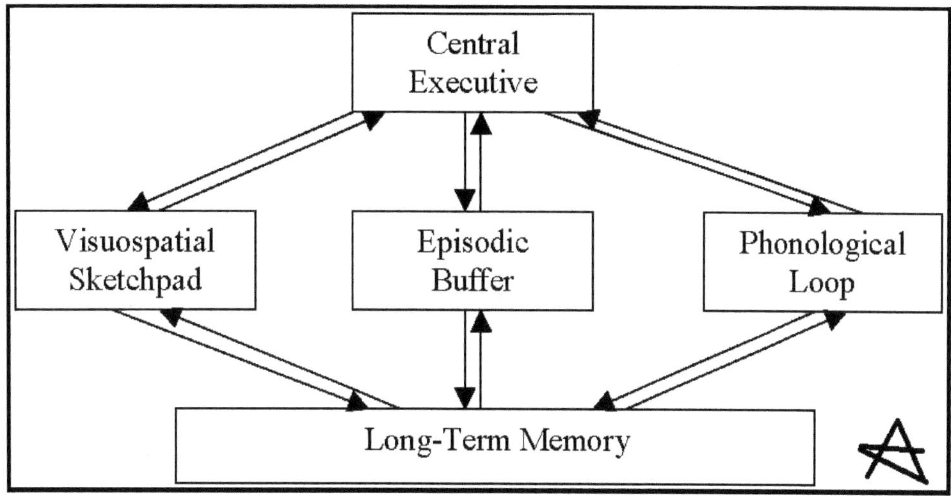

FIG-1.20:Baddeley and Hitch Model of Working Memory

Alan Baddeley and Graham Hitch proposed the model of working memory back in 1974. They provided an in-depth understanding of the mind and how it processes information. Four more elements are added to further illustrate the information processing theory (Goldstein & Mackewn, 2005), namely:

Central executive – It is considered the control center of the mind where information processes are regulated between various memory stores. It controls and implements the cognitive processes that encode and retrieve information. Additionally, the central executive receives information from the visuospatial sketchpad, episodic buffer, and phonological loop. The frontal lobe of the brain is thought to house the central executive, as this is where all active decisions are processed.

Phonological loop – It works closely with the central executive and holds auditory information. Furthermore, it is composed of two sub-components:

Phonological store – It holds auditory information for a short period.

Articulatory rehearsal process – It stores the information for longer periods of time through rehearsal (Baddeley & Hitch, 2019).

Visuospatial sketch pad – It is considered another part of the central executive that holds spatial and visual information. It helps the mind imagine objects and maneuver through the environment.

Episodic buffer – Baddeley later added the fourth element of the model, which also holds information. It increases the capability of the mind to store information. He believed that the episodic buffer transfers information between short-term memory, perception, and long-term memory. As it is still relatively new, research is still conducted as to its specific mechanisms (Goldstein & Mackewn, 2005).

3.4:Limitations of Information Processing Theory:

FIG-1.21:LIMITATIONS OF INFORMATION PROCESSING THEORY

Just like any theory, the information processing theory has its limitations. While the presented models adequately describe how information is processed, several issues arise as well:

Analogy Between Computer and Human is Limited

The information processing theory likens the mind to a computer due to the following aspects:

Combining or connecting new information with stored information reveals new information that can provide solutions to various problems.

A computer has a central processing unit which has limited computing power. Similarly, the central executive in humans has a limited capacity that affects the human attentional system.

One of the obvious limitations of this analogy is the capacity of the human brain to store information that is on the order of 108432 bits. That means the capacity of human memory is excessively better than a computer's (Wang, Liu, & Wang, 2003). This quantity gap between a computer and a human brain means the latter can accommodate processes that the former simply cannot. Also, the analogy also does not consider the motivational and emotional factors that affect a human's cognition.

The Models Assume Serial Processing

Existing models of information processing theory assume serial processing, which means one process needs to be completed before the next process begins. This is very similar to how a computer functions, hence the analogy.

However, the mind is capable of parallel processing, which means simultaneous processing of various inputs with varying quality (Laberge & Samuels, 1974). Such ability of the human brain depends on the processes needed to accomplish a task and/or the amount of practice and the ability of the individual.

For example, a touch typist is able to read passages while typing them on the keyboard. On the other hand, a novice typist would focus on a letter or a word at a time.

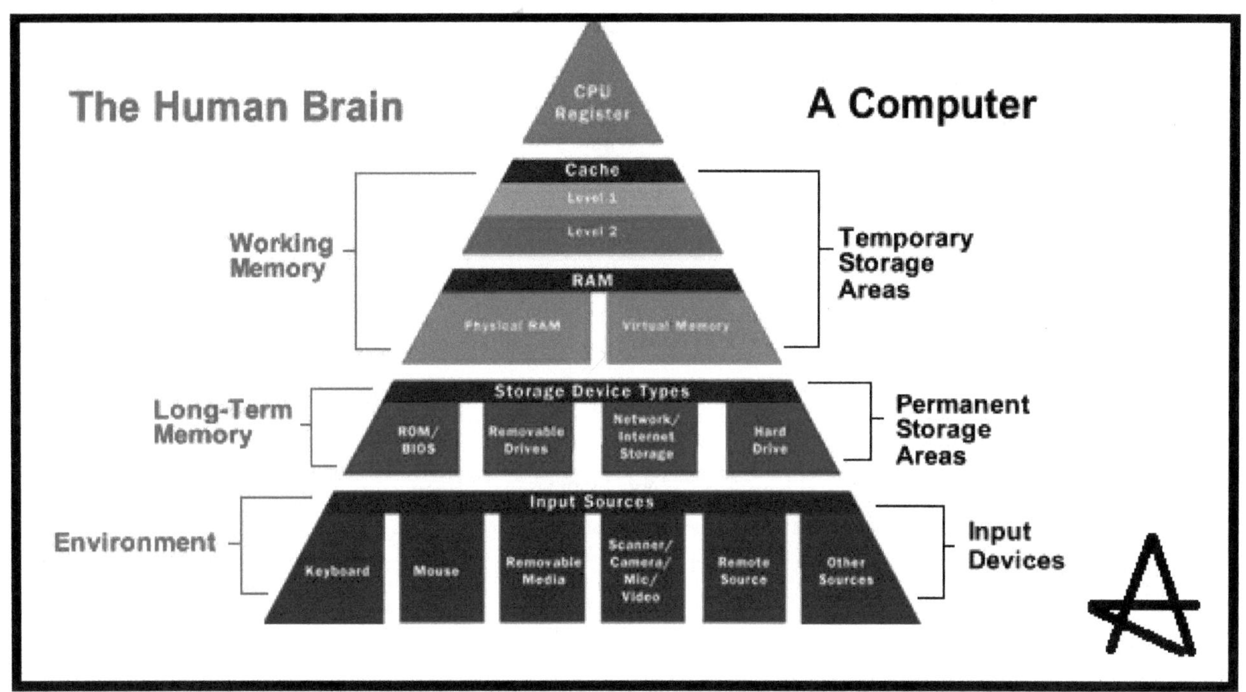

FIG-1.22:ANALOGY BETWEEN HUMAN MIND & COMPUTER

CHAPTER FOUR

CHALLENGES

4.1:CONFUSED MIND:

Humans are naturally trapped in existential thoughts of food,water & reproduction.Similarly most of the students are being trapped in some sort of confusions and are unable to think freely.so the first challenge is a confused mind.

Generally students have an unstable mind,their brainwave frequencies changes abruptly and these changes are so fast that students are unable to gradually progress and learn effectively.

FIG-1.23:CONFUSED MIND

4.2:BELIEF SYSTEMS:

At every time in our life we are working under some sort of patterns. these entire patterns are stored within our memories and our **"MIND-BRAIN SYSTEM"** gets emotionally attached to our past.and its hard to get rid of our past experiences.because of this its said that you have to **bear the brunt** of your karmas.as you can't manipulate the patterns even if you try.

For solving problems you have to modulate yourself according to the

FIG-1.24: BELIEF SYSTEMS

4.3:MULTI-TASKING:

Normally humans are unable to do multitasking or parallel processing.but during information processing multitasking is required as with too much gap,the patterns of information processing gets altered and hence we are unable to generate some productive result.

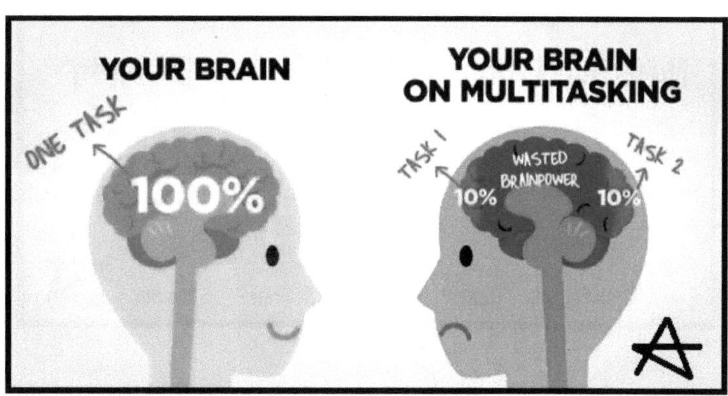

FIG-1.25: INEFFECTIVE MULTI-TASKING

FIG-1.26: INEFFECTIVE MULTI-TASKING

4.4:NEGATIVE EMOTIONS:

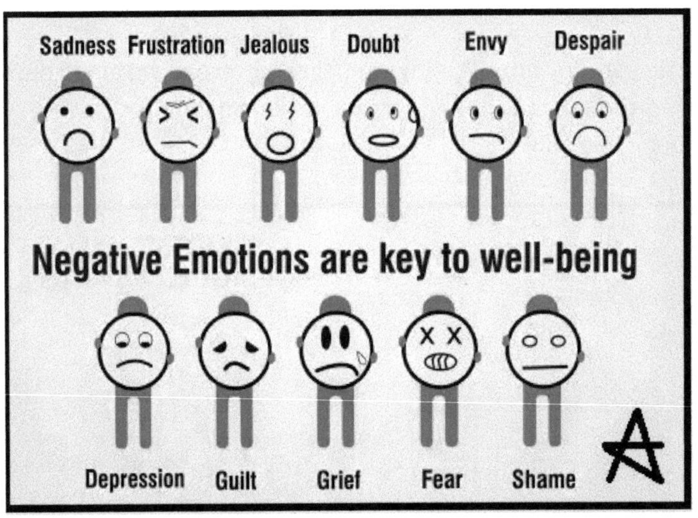

FIG-1.27: NEGATIVE EMOTIONS

FIG-1.28: NEGATIVE EMOTIONS

A student generally feel negative emotions like Tension, lack of confidence, less preparation, excitement, and these negative emotions interferes with the abilty of students to learn and perform.

4.5:TIME MANAGEMENT:

FIG-1.29: TIME MANAGEMENT

All the competitive exams are time bound exams.For example in NEET ,there are about 6000 pages and out of these exams questions are asked only from 20-25 pages.and that too uring 3 hours.so time manegement plays a very crucial role.A student has to manage his time daily to complete the daily targets,and he has to follow this pattern for at least 1 or 2 years.

But generally students are not good in time management.so its a big challenge for the students.

4.6: NEGATIVE MARKING:

FIG-1.30: NEGATIVE MARKING

Most of the competitive exams are based on mcqs having negative marking.so generally students are afraid of negative marking.

4.7: MANIPULATION BASED QUESTIONS:

generally the questions asked in competitive exams are multi-conceptual and tricky and there is a pattern to decode such questions only those students which have practiced a lot of multi-conceptual problems can solve these questions.

FIG-1.31: MANIPULATION BASED QUESTIONS

4.8:LACK OF STUDY PLANS & STRATEGIES:

Generally students study randomly without making a strtaegy.As the exam syllabus is quite wide so most of the students gets distracted on the way and are unable to stick to their plan and gets distracted or over excited about the exam.while if you grdually work with your study plans its quite easy to prepare and perform effectively.

FIG-1.32: LACK OF STUDY PLANS & STRATEGIES

4.9:EXAM ANXIETY:

FIG-1.33: EXAM ANXIETY

Most of the students are afraid of solving questions because solving a question involves use of different parts of the brain and to execute these different processes we need to use more energy or more specifically higher brainwwave frequency.

our brain activates the flight mode and we have to work a lot to dominate the flight mode of the mind.This creates anxiety and as an impact students feel uncomfortable during exams.

4.10:LACK OF EXAM MANAGEMENT SKILLS:

As exam syllabus is quite wide in competitive exams so its necessary to develop exam management skills like random order questions and solution optimization.sometimes some questions asked in the compititive exams are quite tricky and its not easy to solve them for anybody.

The sharp students leave these questions at first hand and try to solve other questions which they can easily solve.while other students gets trapped in tricky questioons and waste much time and end up being frustrted and demotivated which affects their further performance.

FIG-1.34: LACK OF EXAM MANAGEMENT SKILLS

CHAPTER FIVE

SOLUTIONS

4.1:SOLUTIONS TO CONFUSED MIND:

4.1.1:LEARN TO FOCUS:

The ability to focus is the solution to confused mind.hence students must try to learn how to focus.There exist **"law of attraction"**,you get on what you **"FOCUS"**.

FIG-1.35: LEARN TO FOCUS

Focusing can be developed with gradual training programs.You can start with the habit of focusing on a single task and then gradually learn the art of focusing on multiple tasks forming a pattern of switching the focus between different tasks.

For focusing just manage your energy, not your time. If a task requires your full focus, then do it when you have the corresponding energy for it.As energy is fundamental behind any task so the first priority is to focus on energy not on time.just focus on energy and rest will be managed automatically.

FIG-1.36: LEARN TO FOCUS

4.1.2:.LEARN TO DOMINATE FLIGHT MODE:

Human brain is **by default** settled to make life comfortable,so whenever we see a problem the first reaction of the brain is to activate **flight mode** in which we feel **fear,anxiety,depression,low feelings** and we will try to **run away** from the situation.

FIG-1.37: LEARN TO DOMINATE FLIGHT MODE

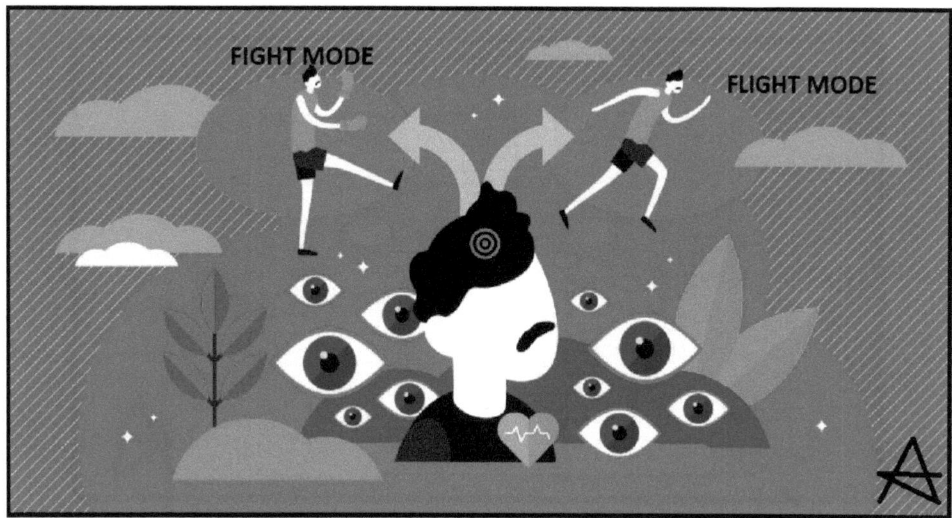

FIG-1.38: LEARN TO DOMINATE FLIGHT MODE

Generally when a student see a problem asked in **competitIve exam**,the first reaction of his brain is to activate the **flight mode**.he will feel **fear,anxiety,depression,hurry** and will not be able to solve the problem.so before starting preparation make sure that you have dominated the flight mode of mind.

4.1.3:DEVELOP A STRONG WILL POWER:

Strong will power is the foundation behind dominating the flight mode of mind. every achievement is possible only after dominating the flight mode.untill we are unable to dominate the flight mode we are unable to achieve anything and will just keep on making stories and excuses.so before starting preparation of any competitive exam make sure that you have guts to dominate the flight mode of mind.

Competitive exam are often based on manipulated or twisted questions and you can't solve them in a straighforward way.you have to switch between different parts of the brain to solve a particular question and for that you need to have a strong will power so as to manage the swiching between different parts of the brain.

FIG-1.39: DEVELOP A STRONG WILL POWER

4.1.4:.LEARN BRAINWAVE FREQUENCY MODULATION:

Different parts of the brain operates at different frequencies.The variation of brainwaves can be measured with electroencephalograph,which measures brainwaves of different frequencies.To measure these frequencies,Electrodes are placed on different parts of the scalp to detect and record the electrical impulses in the brain.

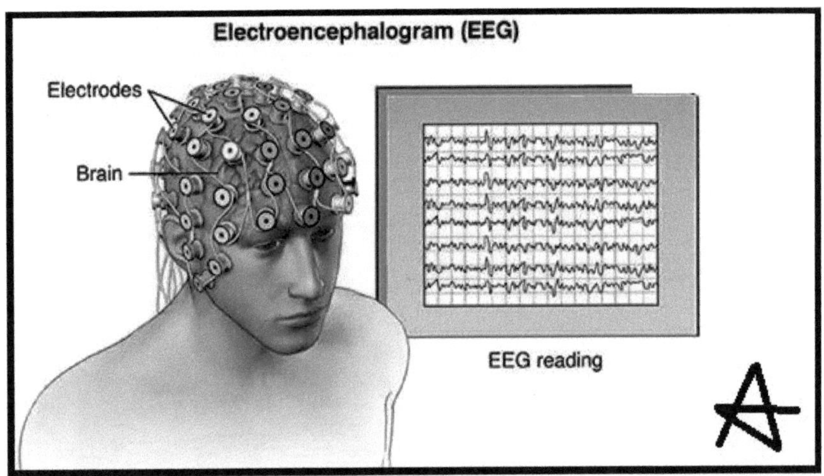

FIG-1.40: LEARN BRAINWAVE FREQUENCY MODULATION

A wave is basically a disturbance.generally electromagnetic impulses can be analysed as a superposition of sinusoidal variations of electromagnetic fields.The number of cycles completed by a wave in 1 second is called frequency.It is similar to the frequency of radio stations to listen to a specific station you need to tune your radio at that specific frequency.

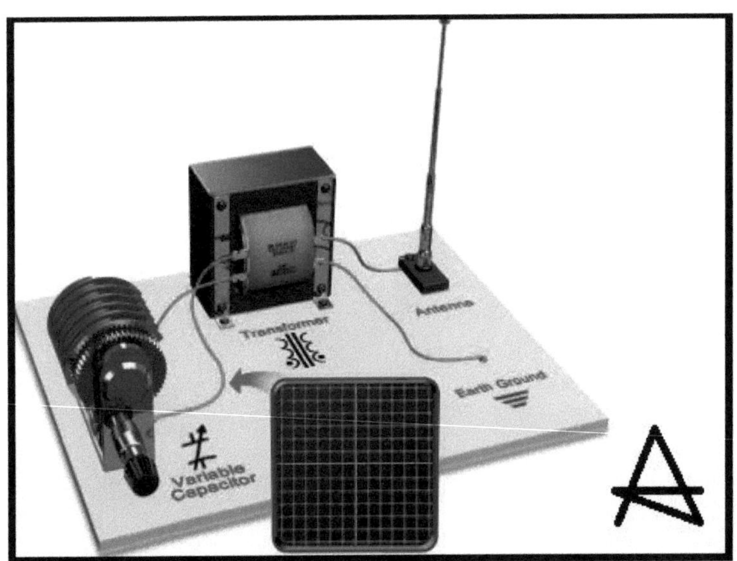

FIG-1.41: LEARN BRAINWAVE FREQUENCY MODULATION

when you solve a particular question your "MIND-BRAIN SYSTEM" follows a certain pattern in which you need to use different functions of the brain.These different functions are activated at different brain-wave frequencies.and if we are not able to operate our brain at some frequencies then tha pattern of solving problems is not completed and we won't be able to get the solution and answer.

Generally the brainwave frequency spectrum of the EEG can be analysed in terms of frequency bands like-

1.Gamma waves(frequency greater than 30Hz)

2.Beta waves (frequency between 13-30Hz)

3.Alpha waves (frequency between 8-12 Hz)
4.Theta waves (frequency between 4-8 Hz)
5. Delta(frequency less than 4 Hz)

It has been experimentally observed that a good problem solver/intelligent student operates his brain at a frequency of 13 Hz.If your brain is having deficieny of 13Hz frequency then you won't be able to develop yourself into an intelligent student and a good problem solver which will ultimately affect your performance and success in competitive exam.

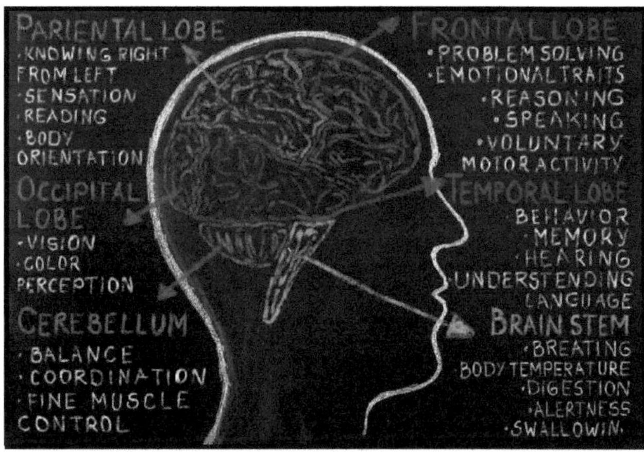

FIG-1.42: DIFFERENT BRAIN PARTS

FIG-1.43: BRAINWAVE FREQUENCY MODULATION

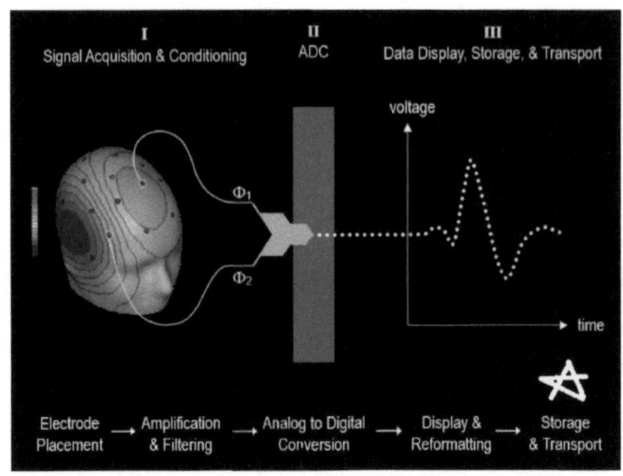

FIG-1.44: BRAINWAVE FREQUENCY MODULATION

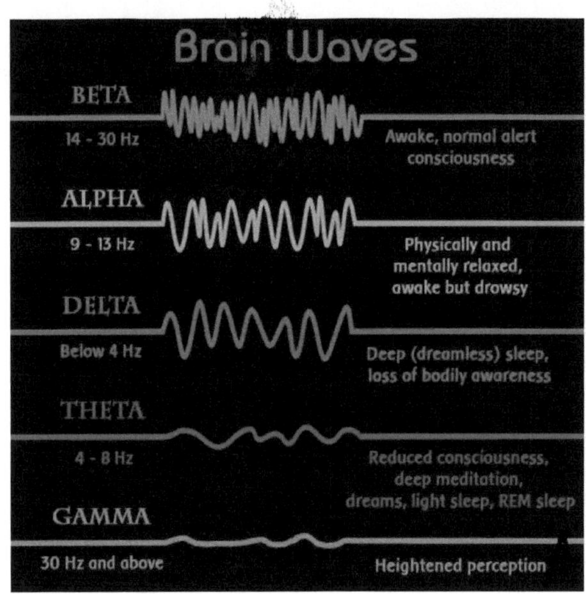

FIG-1.45: BRAINWAVE FREQUENCY MODULATION

4.1.5:. LEARN MULTI-TASKING:

Questions asked in **competiitve exams** are often based on **manipulation** and use of **different parts** of the **brain**.So you have to use different parts of the **brain simultaneously.**

FIG-1.46: LEARN MULTI-TASKING

By default human brain is able to focus on a single task at a single time,we just need to manage the switching between different tasks and develop some sort of **transition time** so that we are able to switch between different functions of the brain simultaneously.

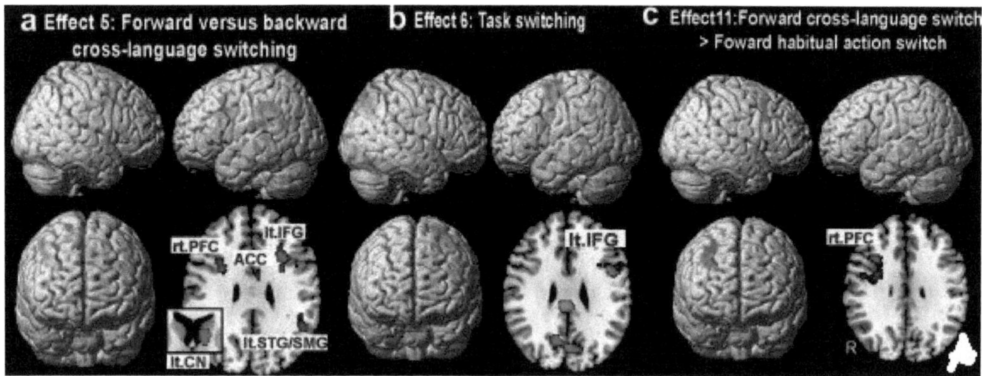

FIG-1.47: NEURAL ACTIVITY IN HUMAN BRAIN

hence to be an expert in **problem solving** you must be able to use different parts of the brain in a pattern having very short time gap between different brain part activation.This seems to be a very challenging task,but it can be systematically learnt with a **gradual training program.**

FIG-1.47: LEARN MULTI-TASKING

FIG-1.48: LEARN MULTI-TASKING

4.1.6:.TRAIN YOUR BRAIN:

Normally when a student prepares for competitive exams,he just think about books,notes,questions but he pays no attention to his brain.he think that just learn the answer of some questions and you will be able to crack competitive exams but it is not so.you have to train your brain in actual exam environment so that you can adapt to it and can perform better in it.

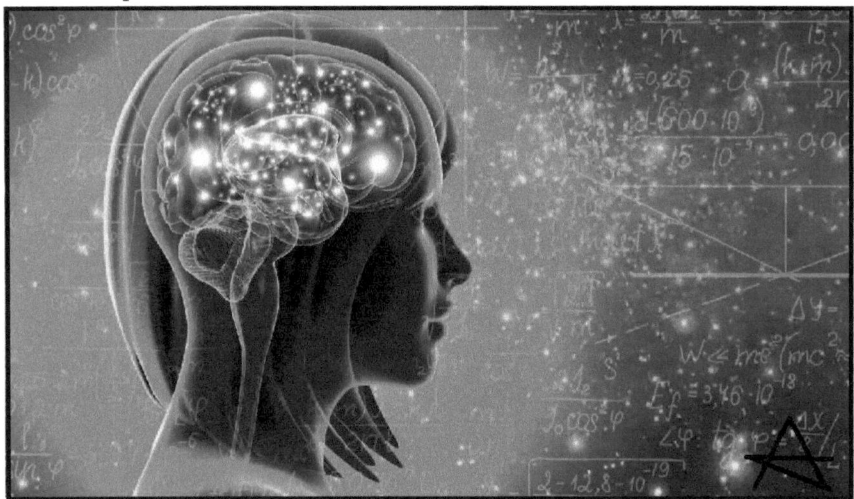

FIG-1.49: TRAIN YOUR BRAIN

there are many ways to train your brain for better performance in competitive exams like:

1. learn new things:

Normally a student like to do the same things and avoid learning new things,when we learn something new then new neural connections are developed and we learn the habit of adapting to new situations.today's Competitive exams are becoming tougher day by day and only those students are capable to crack it who have the capacity to learn new concepts quickly and implement them in exam..

2. Practice mental exercises:

Mental exercises stimulates your brain cells and develops new neural connections which helps in performing better in exams.hence you must practice mental exercises

Solving puzzles,playing mind games,decoding patterns are some of the ways to ensure mental developments.

3.Revise your lessons:

Revision strengthens your neural pathways and ensures effective retention in exams hence you must revise your lessons so that you can recall them as and when needed in competitive exams.

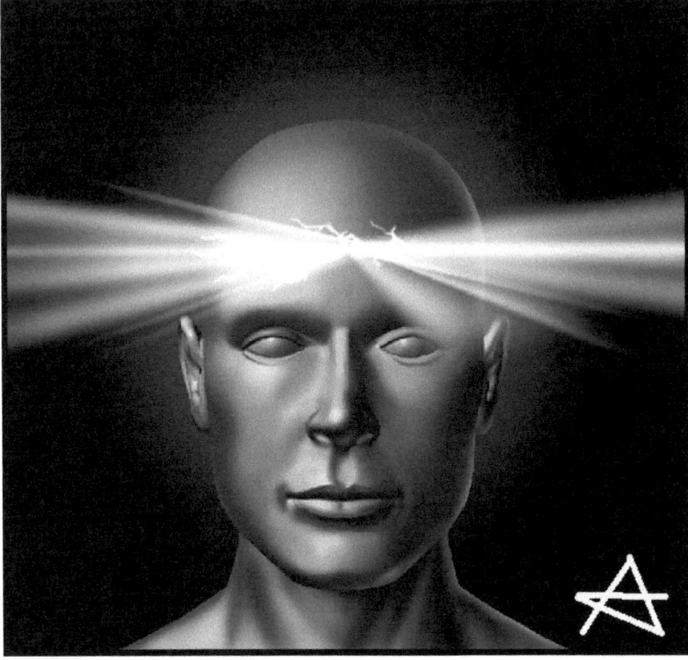

FIG-1.50: TRAIN YOUR BRAIN

4.2:SOLUTIONS TO CONSERVATIVE BELIEF SYSTEMS:

1.FIND SOURCE OF YOUR BELIEF SYSTEM?

Belief systems are based on what we have experienced in our life,but beliefs may not be true in every situation.For example:the belief of non violence is true when you wish to explore higher dimensions of life beyond survival,but its false when a goon is about to kill you for your money.in order to save your life you can take any step,its legitimate and valid in legal perspectives also.so belief systems are time dependent,during favourible time its good to follow belief systems but with change in time beliefs have to be changed to lead for a better future.

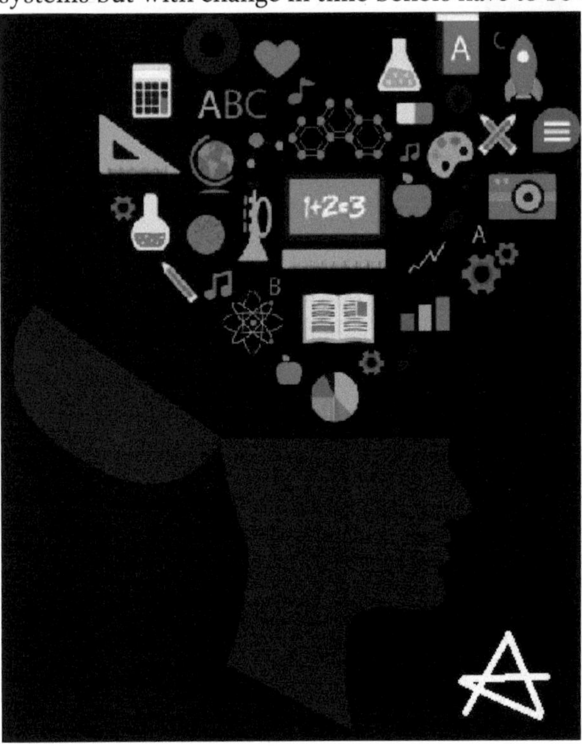

FIG-1.51: FIND SOURCE OF YOUR BELIEF SYSTEM?

2.TRY TO THINK BEYOND INFORMATION:

Just observe your surroundings with silent observations and try to think beyond information.you will feel that the entire universe is following a pattern and all these patterns are destined to the development of everybody.

FIG-1.52: TRY TO THINK BEYOND INFORMATION

3.MAKE FRIENDS HAVING OPPOSITE NATURE AS THAT OF YOU:

What we consider ourself is due to what we have experienced in life,but we may not be able to contemplate any event in all the possible dimensions and our experience and its interpretation may be biased.There exist hidden dimensions of a particular event.

so things in which you are not comfortable also exist and you must be able to accept this harsh truth that you are not "All" that exist,what you think of yourself is a miniscule of what "exist".

so there must be somebody who reminds you that you are on the route of expanding consciousness,all the events that comes

FIG-1.53: MAKE FRIENDS HAVING OPPOSITE NATURE AS THAT OF YOU

4.3:SOLUTIONS TO NEGATIVE EMOTIONS:

Generally when a student tries to solve a problem,he has to encounter negative emotions.Negative emotions disturbs our **"MIND-BRAIN SYSTEM"** and interfere in its capability to function properly.hence its necessary to get rid of negative emotions.

FIG-1.54: SOLUTIONS TO NEGATIVE EMOTIONS

1. **PRACTICE MEDITATION:**Meditation is a way to get rid of your negative energy and emotions.

FIG-1.55: PRACTICE MEDITATION

2.PRACTICE YOGA:

FIG-1.56: PRACTICE YOGA

Yoga is about interconnecting your diverging energies to form a focused and converging mental state

The following yoga poses must be practiced for clearing negative energies

1. Marjaryasana:The Cat-to-Cow pose is beneficial as it calms the mind, relieves stress amd releases tension in the shoulders and neck.

2.Urdhva Mukha Svanasana: This pose is not mentioned often but it is considered to be the best yoga poses for clearing negative energies. It helps in fighting depression and fatigue.B) .

3.SUKHASANA:The "Easy Pose" is one that helps in bringing peace to the helm. A forward bend, when practiced correctly, can aid in bringing calm.

3. ORGANISE YOUR WORK SPACE:

FIG-1.57: ORGANISE YOUR WORK SPACE

Organise your work space.organised workspace radiated positive vibrtaions which stimulates you to do better work.

4.DEVELOP YOUR POSITIVE ENERGY FIELDS:

Normally a student has unstable energy fields which changes with time so its extremly important to develop positive energy fields so that you can cross the threshhold of negative emotions.

The best way to develop positive energy fields is to practice a mantra at least 21 times a day.

FIG-1.58: DEVELOP YOUR POSITIVE ENERGY FIELDS

4.4:TIME MANAGEMENT:

FIG-1.59: TIME MANAGEMENT

As all the competitive exams are time based exams so its very crucial to manage your time.This skill can be learnt over time by gradually practicising a lot of mock tests.. students become more focused and productive when we are good in time management.It increases our Productivity which leads to better performance and hence better results.

Some benifits of time management are:

1.Focused Mind-brain system

2. Enhanced Productivity

3.Comfortable working

4.Self motivated personality

Some of the techniques to develop time management skills are:

1. Start with time-bound studies:

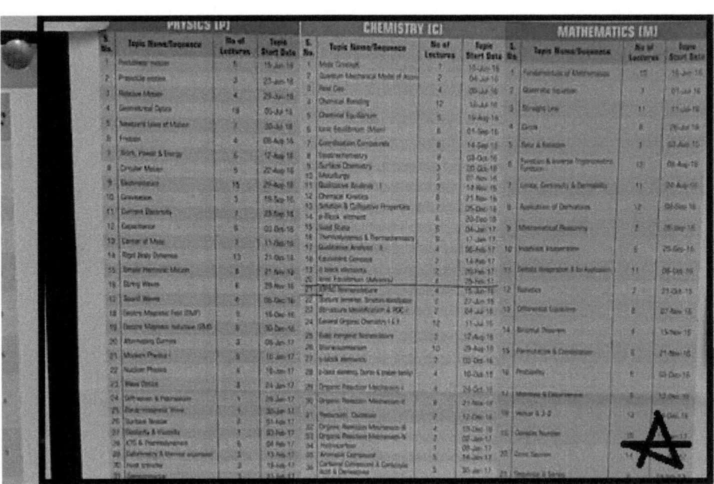

FIG-1.60: Start with time-bound studies

Before studying make sure it is time bounded.For example:assign time to each chapter.if you are studying kinematics set a time limit for it.lets say 3 days then plan for each day that what you will complete in each day in this way you can prepare better and can actually prepare rather than acting to prepare.

2. Practice Decision Making:

FIG-1.61: Practice Decision Making

For developing time management you must be good at decision making because at times you need to make strong decisions about what to do at a given instant of time.and this decision making can't be developed instantly but by gradual practise over an enhanced duration of time

3. Develop the habit of plan making:

FIG-1.62: Develop the habit of plan making

Time management skills can't be developed in 2 minutes.It takes a considerable amount of time to develop these skills,hence you must develop a habit of making plan by working for at least 21 days.

FIG-1.63: 21 DAYS HABIT

All the competitive exams are time bound exams.For example in NEET ,there are about 6000 pages and out of these exams questions are asked only from 20-25 pages.and that too uring 3 hours.so time manegement plays a very crucial role.A student has to manage his time daily to complete the daily targets,and he has to follow this pattern for at least 1 or 2 years.But generally students are not good in time management.so its a big challenge for the students to crack competitive exams.

4.6: NEGATIVE MARKING:

FIG-1.64: NEGATIVE MARKING

Negative marking is a major concern in competitive exams.so to get rid of negative marks you must be an expert in problem solving here are some of the steps to develop msharp problem solving skills-

1. Accept the problem:

The first step in having a sharp problem solving skill is to accept the problem.Generally the first problem which a student face while solving a problem is a flight mode activation which results in negative feelings like fear,anxiety,anger,depression,hurry,inability to focus etc.

2. Design a solution:

The next step in problem solving is to design the solution.try to connect the problem and the solution.use imaginations,information anything but connect the problem with the solution.

3. work on each step:

After designing the stepwise solution work on each step and make sure that you complete each step successfully

4. Take proper decision:

develop a sharp decision making habit.In the process of problem solving the entire game is centred around making effective decisions.So you must have the art of taking optimal decisions when placed in tough situations.when solving a complex problem in competitive exams,a student generally faces emotional distractions and he has to choose the most optimised options out of available options.

5. work on your decisions:

after making a decision,the next step is to implement your decisions.

6. Analyse the output:

Analyse the output.see if you have come to the correct answer or not,if not then replan the enire solution and check where is the problem.

4.7:SOLUTIONS TO MANIPULATION BASED PROBLEMS:

Generally the questions asked in competitive exams are **multi-conceptual** and **tricky** and there is a pattern to decode such questions only those students which have practiced a lot of multi-conceptual problems can solve these questions.

for solving manipulation based questions,you need to disintegrate the multi-conceptual question into a combination of different concepts and then work on each concept independently and finally compile the total solutions by integrating the results of different concepts.

4.8:SOLUTIONS TO LACK OF STUDY PLANS & STRATEGIES:

1.DEVELOP STUDY PLANS:

Develop daily,weekly,monthly,quarterly,half yearly and yearly study plans by carefully dividing the syllabus into suitable parts and then systematically working on each part.Have a detailed syllabus of the competitive exam and develop plans about how to complete the entire syllabus timely,revision plans

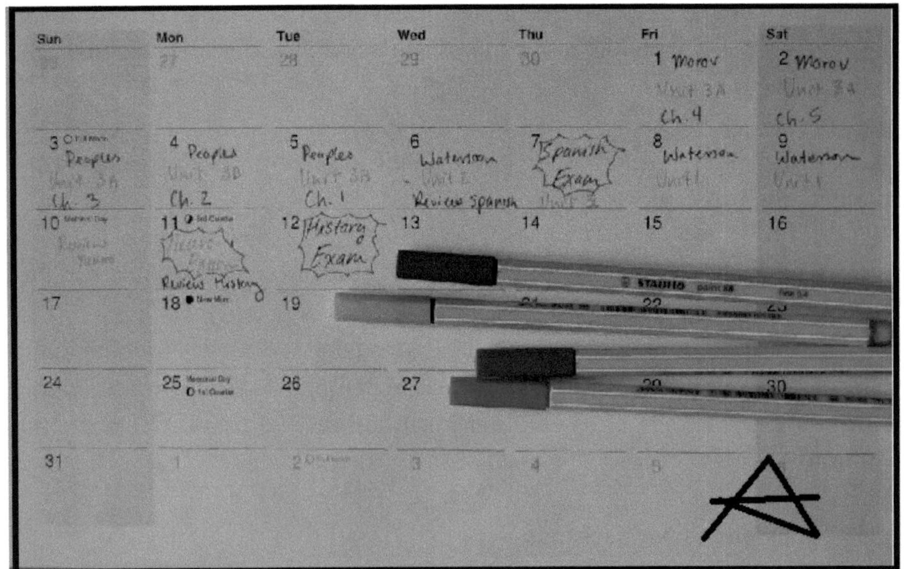

FIG-1.65: DEVELOP STUDY PLANS

2.DEVELOP STRATEGIES:

FIG-1.66: DEVELOP STRATEGIES

Develop exam strategies.give a lot of mock tests so as to make yourself adaptive to the high pressure exam conditions.implement these strategies and make sure that you are able to dominate the flight mode of mind as explained earlier.

Analyse your performance and make strtaegies to have a better performance.

9:EXAM ANXIETY:

FIG-1.67:EXAM ANXIETY

Its very natural to suffer from exam anxiety if you have not adapted to the exam environment.the best strategies to deal with the exam anxiety is to practice a lot of mock tests and face the exam rather than being deviated due to high pressure exam condiitons.There are certain ways to deal with the exam anxiety these are:

1.Practice mental simulation of high pressure exam environment:

FIG-1.68:Practice mental simulation of high pressure exam environment

visualize that you have started solving the questions in exam and face the emotional conflicts within you.The first reaction of your "**MIND-BRAIN SYSTEM**" is to activate the flight mode so that you can be comfortable.its necessary to survive but if you think beyond survival

FIG-1.69:Practice mental simulation of high pressure exam environment

2.Don't change your study schedule during the last night before exam:

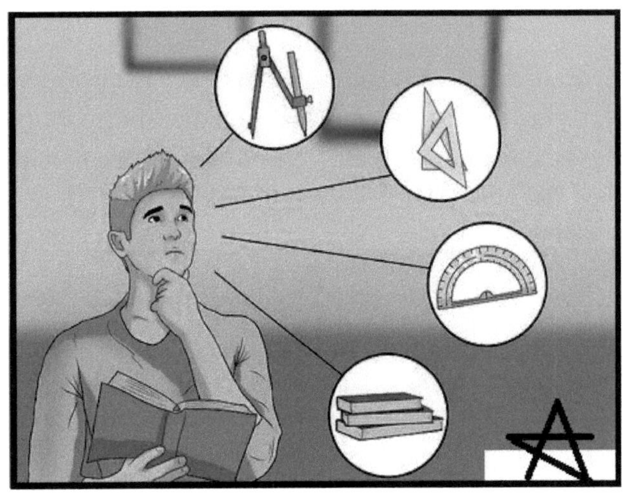

FIG-1.70:Don't change your study schedule during the last night before exam

Sure, you're going to do some last-minute cramming the night before a test. Just don't do it with the aid of quarts of coffee or tea. The reason: Caffeine adds to stress. Gulp some caffeine and, come test-time, you may be too wired to focus on the job in front of you.

3.Take some light food before exam:

Light food make sure that you don't feel sleepy as it is easy to digest and requires less energy so it saves your precious energy which can be used for better performance hence make sure that you take a light food before exam.

FIG-1.71:Take some light food before exam

For a couple of hours before a test, stay away from food or, if you must, just sample some. Eat and you might get drowsy. Your digestive system will be competing with your brain for oxygen-rich blood. Better than eating, take a walk to get that blood moving rapidly through your body.

4.Be in focused state of mind:

Human mind is generally in monkey-mind state that is it keeps on changing randomly.This problem can be resolved by practicising a focused state of mind which can be learnt by gradual meditation programs.

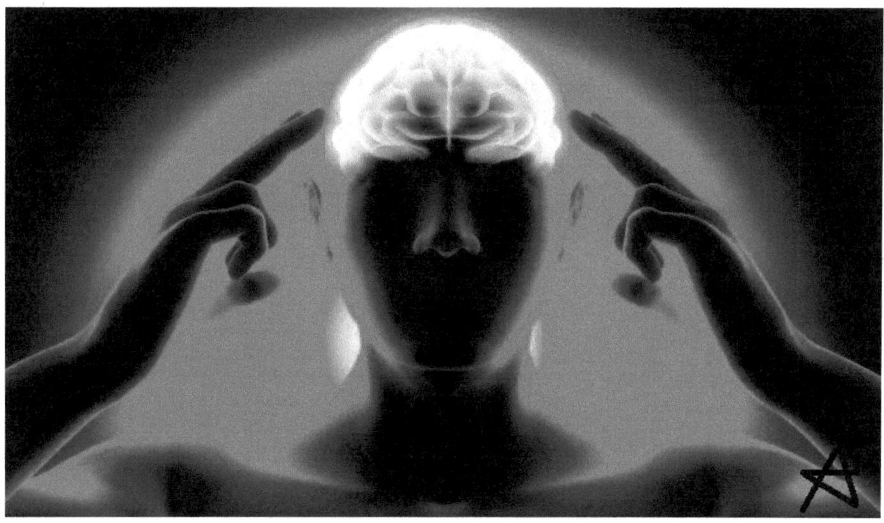

FIG-1.72:Be in focused state of mind

5.Increase the preparation time of exam:

FIG-1.73:Increase the preparation time of exam

Start preparing for the exam as soon as possible.The topper students in any competitive exam starts preparing well in advance and as early as class 5 so they have at least 7 years of preparation to develop the mental skills for competitive exams.so they have a prolonged time and can reduce the anxiety level very much.

6.Improve your memory power:

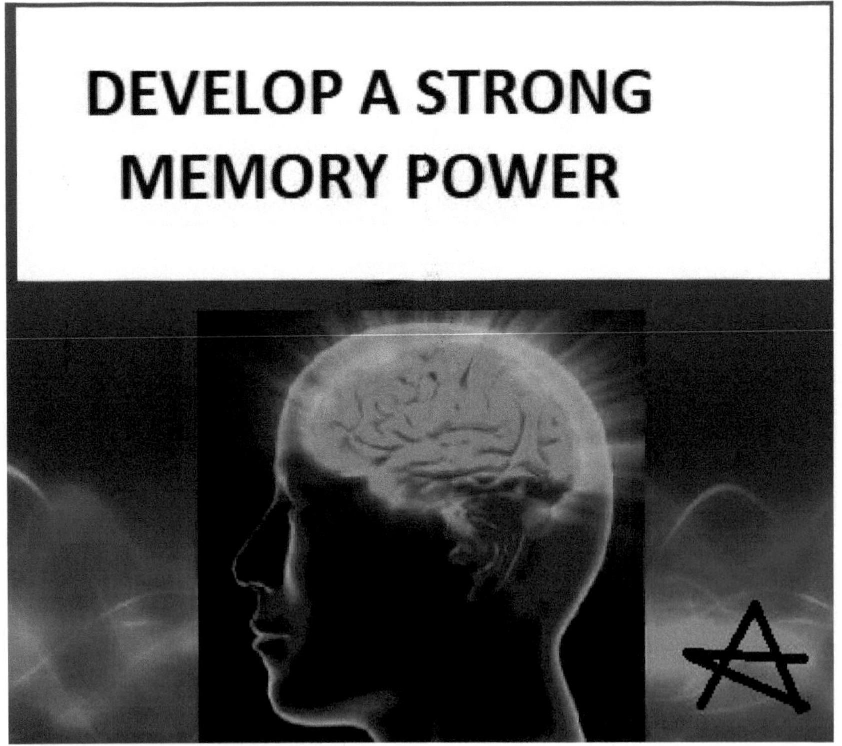

FIG-1.74:Improve your memory power

Competitive exams are mostly based on memory power along with problem solving skills and emotional management skills during exam.The root cause of exam anxiety is weak memory power.when we are unable to retrieve information during exam then negtive feelings like hurry,fear,depression etc ar induced which causes exam anxiety and it reduces the performance a lot.

7.Overcome the phobia of solving questions:

FIG-1.75:Overcome the phobia of solving questions

Most of the students are **afraid of solving questions** because solving a question involves use of different parts of the brain and to execute these different processes we need to use more energy or more specifically higher brainwwave frequency.

our brain activates the flight mode and we have to work a lot to dominate the flight mode of the mind.This creates anxiety and as an impact students feel uncomfortable during exams.

4.10:SOLUTIONS TO LACK OF EXAM MANAGEMENT SKILLS:

1.DON'T HAVE A PRE-BIASED MENTALITY TOWARD EXAM:

FIG-1.76:DON'T HAVE A PRE-BIASED MENTALITY TOWARD EXAM

normally students practice questions and start to think that they can solve any question.Thats not true.you can perfectly solve a question when you have practices its pattern and all the relevant information concerned with the question are stored in your **"MIND-BRAIN SYSTEM"**.if a question involves information which is not in your **"MIND-BRAIN SYSTEM"** then you won't be able to solve it.

so before appearing for any exam be open minded and try to solve the question with your best efforts rather than a pre biased mentality.

FIG-1.77:BE OPEN MINDED TOWARD EXAM

2.Practise a lot of mock tests to develop organisational skills:

Competitive exams are all about organisational skills as there are a lot of tasks needed to successfully crack competitive exams so its very necessary to organise these tasks in proper order so that you can complete all the tasks within the allocated time.

FIG-1.78:Practise a lot of mock tests to develop organisational skills

3.Develop sharp decision making skills:

FIG-1.79: Develop sharp decision making skills

Some questions asked in competitive exams are very tricky and they need a key to solve them or they need a decoding algorithm to solve.The sharp students know this and they attempt such questions only if they can decode the trick of question.otherwise they leave the question and attempt the next questions without being anxious or worried about the tricky question.

they score optimally by carefully choosing which question they can attempt and hence their optimal decision enables themto have optimal performance in the exam.

CHAPTER SIX

MIND PATTERNS

6.1:Patterns in the universe:

Universe is following a pattern,everything ranging from the vibrations of a tiny string as per the "string theory to the expansion of universe is following a pattern or are working under some rigid protocols.in other worlds as everything is fundamentally concerned with the vibrations of the strings,things are different because of difference in frequency of vibrations.

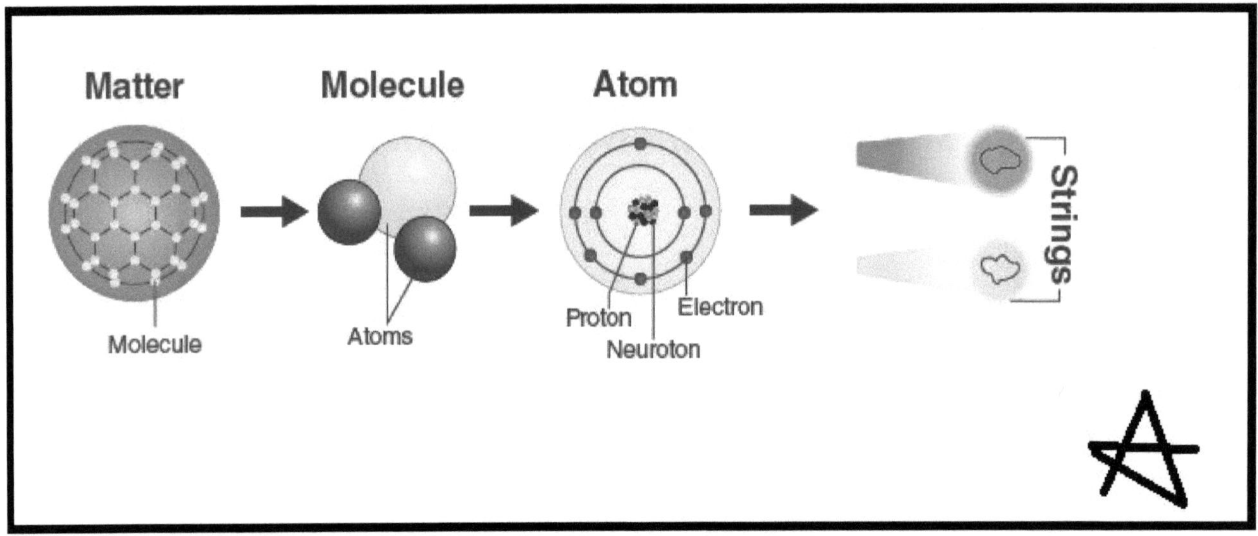

FIG-1.80: Patterns in the universe

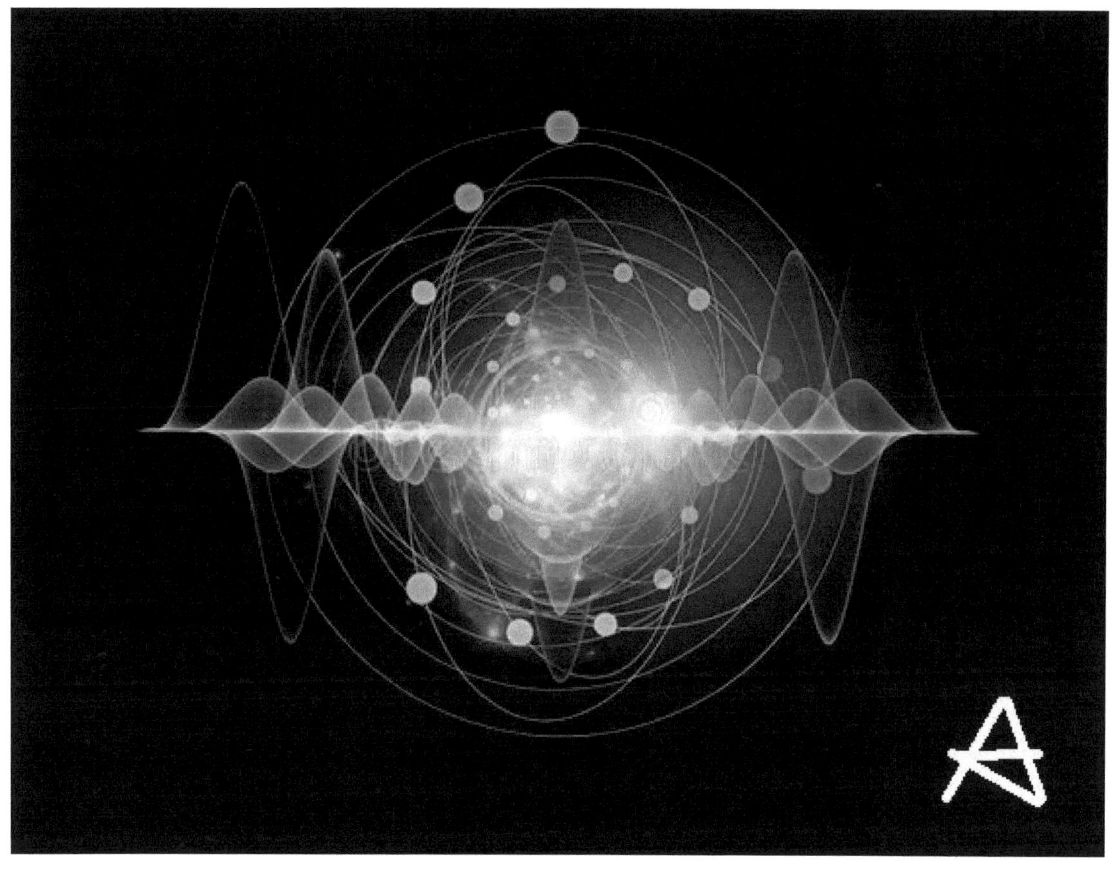

FIG-1.81: PATTERNS OF VIBRATIONS OF A STRING

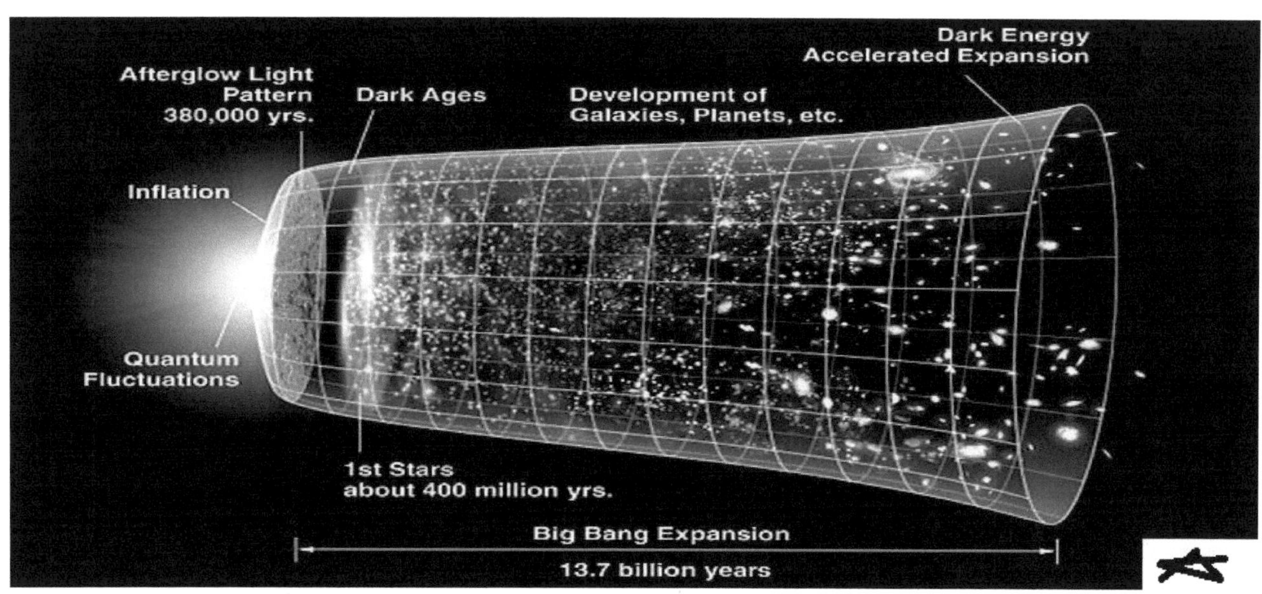

FIG-1.82: PATTERNS OF UNIVERSE

6.2:STUDENT AS A "MIND-BRAIN SYSTEM":

if we observe a student as a "**MIND-BRAIN SYSTEM".**we can certainly say that all the students of a particular class have access to the same teacher or input,but why output is different for different students.

This is because the process is different for different students.Those students who crack the competitive exams use a **different process** than other students and if the unsuccessful students can learn that "**PROCESS**" then they can **also crack** the competitive exam.Apart from process another dimension is **energy**.As while solving a problem in competitive exam you need to use different parts of the brain which involves frequent shift of information access or "**BRAIN-WAVE FREQUENCY MODULATION**",which consumes a lot of energy hence students must also practice a lot on "**BRAIN-WAVE FREQUENCY MODULATION**" for learning the art of adapting to the energy changes while solving a problem.

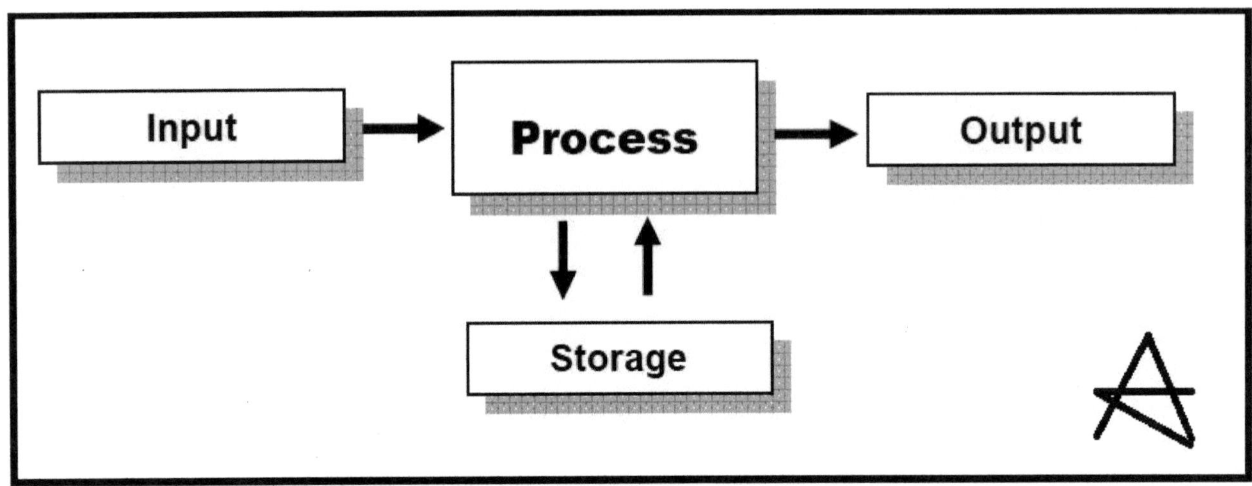

FIG-1.83: STUDENT AS A "MIND-BRAIN SYSTEM"

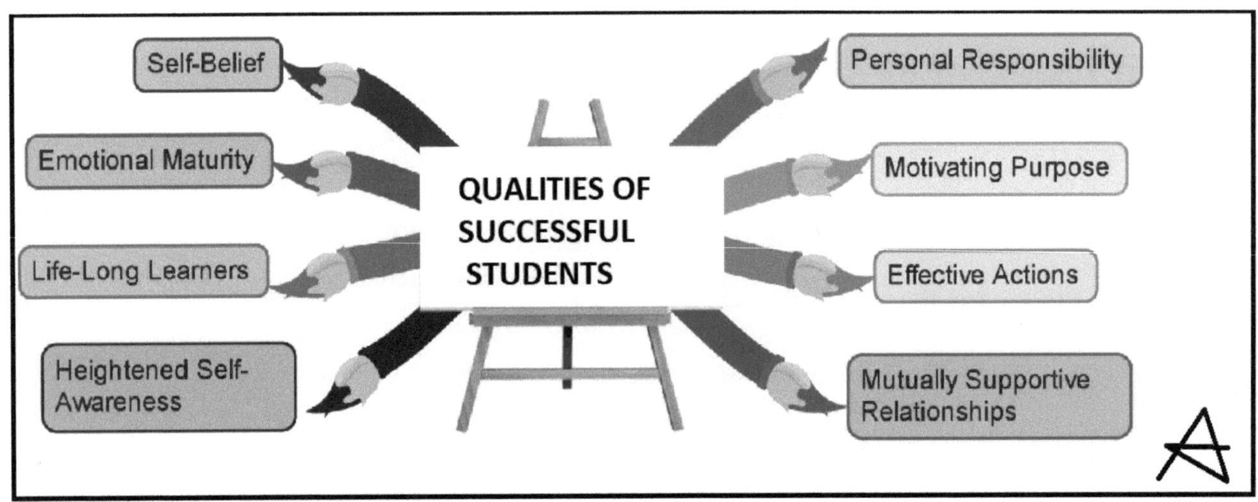

FIG-1.84: STUDENT AS A "MIND-BRAIN SYSTEM"

6.3:MIND PATTERNS FOLLOWED BY A SUCCESSFUL STUDENT:

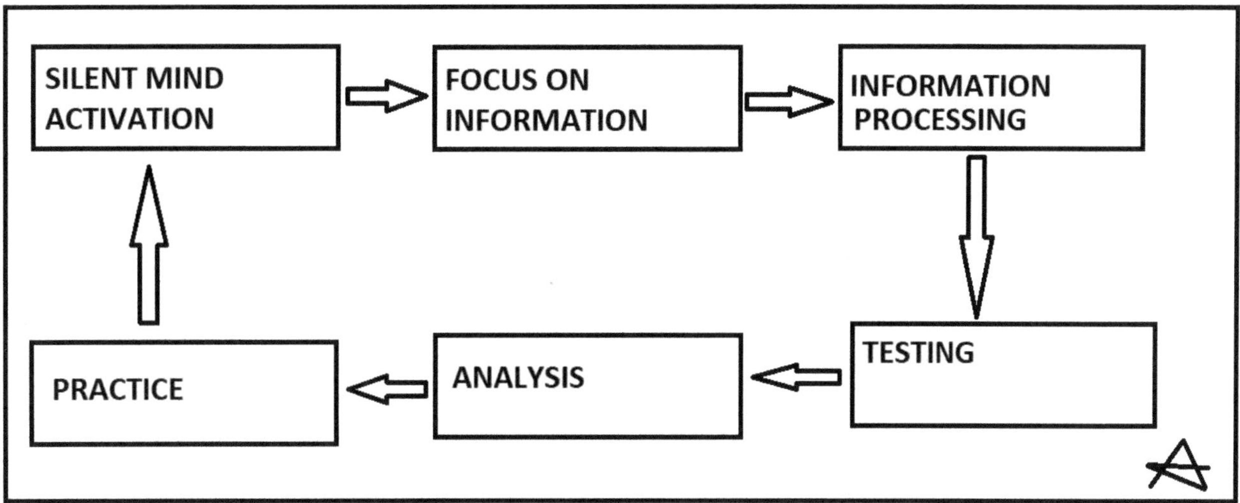

FIG-1.85: MIND PATTERNS FOLLOWED BY A SUCCESSFUL STUDENT

We can say that successfull students perform better than other other students because they use better mind patterns than other students.normally a student is afraid of studies because it involves a lot of energy and mental stress.we have 3 layers of memory which are concerned with conscious,sub-conscious and un conscious mind.Most of the students have just access to the conscious memory which is limited and is of no practical use for performance in competitive exams because the information and the patterns asked in competitive exams are distributed over several years.

FIG-1.86: MIND PATTERNS FOLLOWED BY A SUCCESSFUL STUDENT

for example in **JEE & NEET**,the exam syllabus is distributed for 2 years of class 11 and 12.but it involves alllearning right from class 1.The crucial factor for successfull students are their parents.The active parents know that generally nobody like to study.parents have to struggle a lot with their children to gradually develop their "MIND-BRAIN SYSTEM" and train them for being a better human being.while the inactive parents just think that by just admitting their children to some education system is sufficient to make them successful.thats why most of the students fail in competitive exams.

and its not about failing in competitive exams,its about developing a negative attitude toward life.Such students just blame others for their miserable life.they wish to get all benifits in life but are unable to pay the prize.such students waste their entire life in criticise and blaminfg others and ened up being useless for the nation.

FIG-1.87: A FRUSTRATED STUDENT

However if such students can be trained to develop their **"MIND-BRAIN SYSTEM"** and apply those skills to at least be self dependent.then we can have a better society and can lead toward a developed nation,which is the central philosophy of this book.i hope this book will prove to be a boon to those youths who aspire to crack competitive exams and contribute to the development of self,family,society and the country,leading to the vision of **"DEVELOPING MIND,DEVELOP INDIA"**.

6.4:THEORIES OF MIND:

FIG-1.88: SIGMUND FREUD

According to sigmund Freud,human mind can be studied as unconscious, preconscious, and conscious mind.

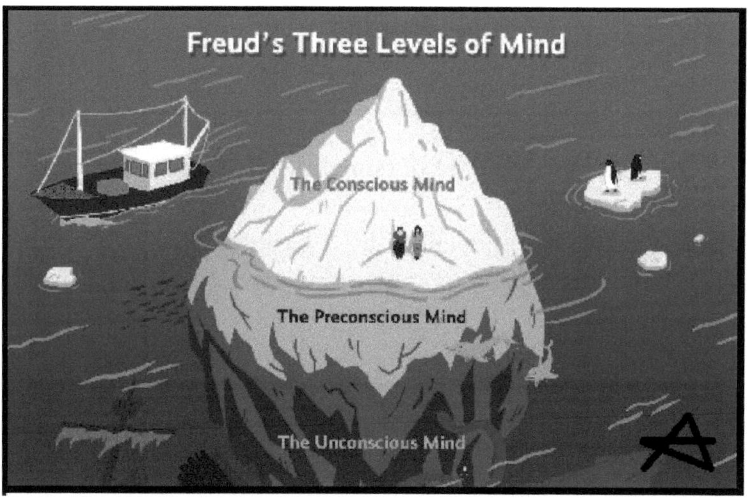

FIG-1.89: THEORIES OF MIND BY SIGMUND FREUD

1.Conscious Mind:

This part of mind is the uppermost or surface layer and it includes information which are necessary to survive.Logical and analytical thinking are controlled by this part of mind.But its the weakest part also thats why we talk big in front of others to impress them but when it comes to implement we can only do what we are capable to do,something more powerful part of the mind which was inactive suddenly becomes active and we are forced to surrender to that powerful part.

when a student start preparing for competitive exams he talk big in front of parents and other people but when he starts solving a question only then his reality can be checked.Most of the students are unable to face the question and feel uncomfortable while solving a question.

only those students are able to crack competitive exams who are able to access the three minds within a very short span of time and in any random order.

lets move to the next level of mind

2.Preconscious/sub conscious Mind:

Preconscious/sub conscious Mind is a buffer for transition between the conscious and unconscious mind.It acts as a storehouse for all the informations which are to be transferred from unconscious to conscious mind.

3.Unconscious Mind:

Unconscious mind contains all the information related to the universe.you just need to access the deepest information.All new inventions or fundamental laws of universe are stored in unconscious mind.but you need to have the right kind of brain to access it.thats why only some people are able to think out of the box and are able to decode the secrets of universe.

6.4:Theory of personalities:

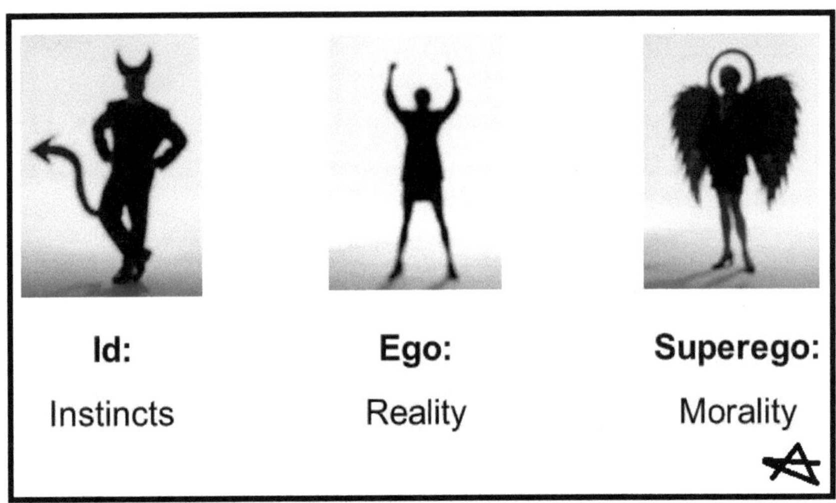

FIG-1.90: Theory of personalities By sigmund freud

As per sigmund freud human beings are influenced by 3 basic personalities or there are 3 different person inside a single person who give him inner suggestions.you can yourself verify the existence of these three different personalities.These are: Id, Ego, and Superego

FIG-1.91: 3 different person inside a person

The Id is concerned with the animal instincts & desires.

The Ego is the practical personality which tries to optimally use resources for a better life.

The Superego is about the morals and ethics.

but one of these personalities dominates over others and that dominated personality decides what type of person you are.

6.4:HOW TO DEVELOP THE MENTAL PATTERN FOR COMPETITIVE EXAMS:

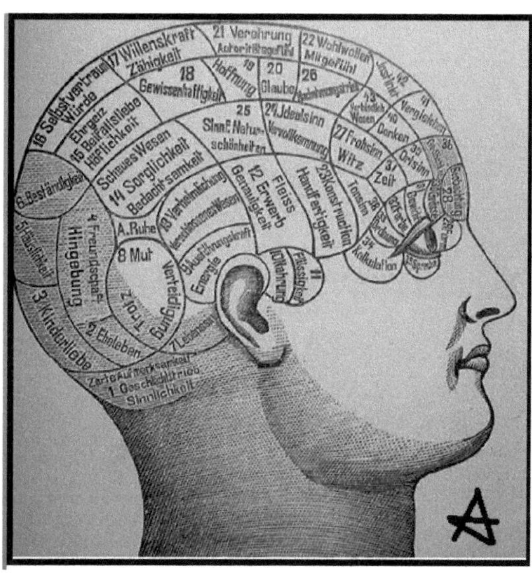

FIG-1.92: MENTAL PATTERN FOR COMPETITIVE EXAMS

Competitive exams is a game of 3 mutually exclusive dimensions.These are-**information,process & energy.**

Most of the students are aware of only the **information** and pay very less attention to the **process and energy**,as an impact of which they just act to prepare but are never mentally preparing for the exam.the real preparation of **competiitve exam** starts after you start solving a **problem** but most of the students are afraid of **solving problems** they **cram theory** and neglect the **problems and the patterns** used to solve the problem, as an impact of which most of the studnets are unable to develop sharp problem solving skills which is a core requirement to crack competitive exams.

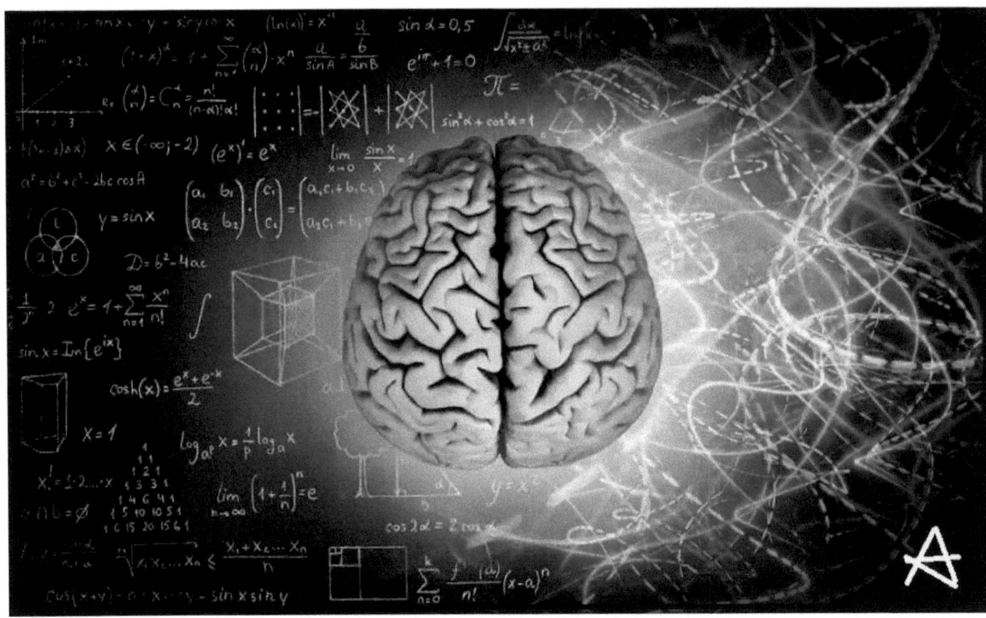

FIG-1.93: LEFT VERSUS RIGHT BRAIN

The problems asked in competitive exams like **JEE & NEET**, are to test your **"MIND-BRAIN SYSTEM"** through multiple dimensions,although for neet and Jee main,if you have practicesd enough and have good command over ncert theory and problems then you can easily crack them with a decent rank however to solve problems for **JEE ADVANCED**,you need to be really sharp and an expert problem solver as there are no fixed patterns or type of questions in **JEE ADVANCED**,you must have an expertise over the subject in order to crack **JEE ADVANCED.**

For cracking a competitive exam you need to access your conscious,sun-conscious and un-conscious mind within a small time gap of a few seconds and it creates a lot of emotional conflicts and issues which leads to fear,anxiety,anger,hurry etc.hence the first task in preparing for competitive exam is tomentlly prepare yourself for the high pressure exam conditions and learn the art of connecting the 3 minds and use them, as a system to solve the problems and finding solutions to the problems within a short time span and high pressure exam conditions.

the general pattern followed by a successful student is shown in the below figure.if you aspire to crack a competitive exam follow the pattern as shown below and practice it agin and again till you are comfortable with it.

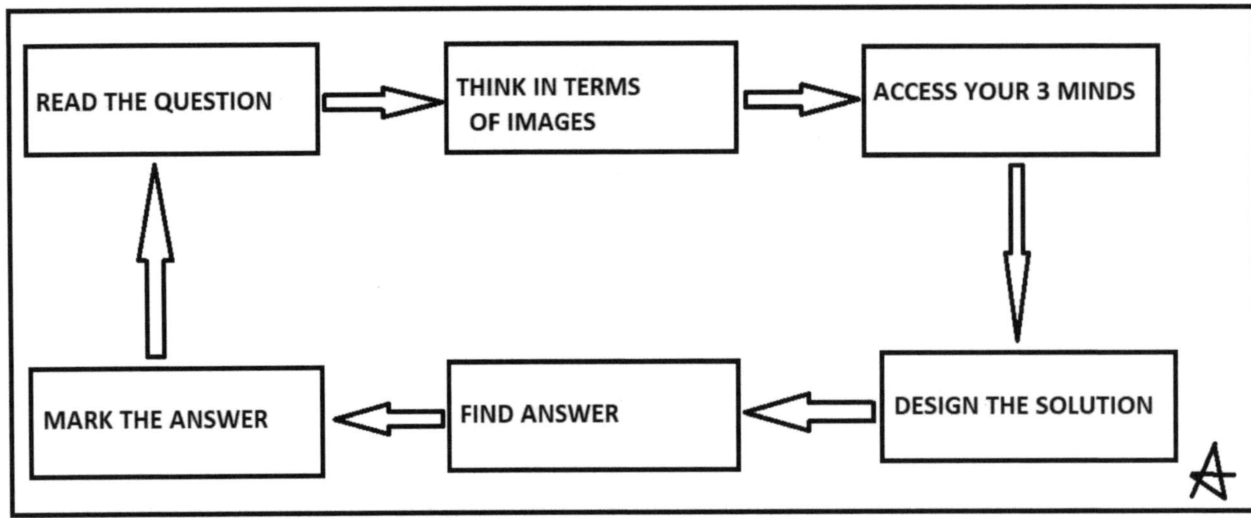

FIG-1.94: MENTAL PATTERN FOR COMPETITIVE EXAMS

CHAPTER SEVEN

THE TRAINING PROGRAM

Make a 21 days training program to evaluate your daily progress and gradually implement the mental pattern in your "MIND-BRAIN SYSTEM"

FIG-1.95: 21 days training program

CHAPTER EIGHT

CONTACT US:

FOR ANY QUERIES OR FEEDBACK CONTACT US AT:
ACHARYAVISHVENDRA@GMAIL.COM

FIG-1.96: CONTACT US

WE HAVE TRIED OUR BEST TO KEEP THIS BOOK ERROR FREE,HOWEVER IF READERS FIND ANY ERROR THEY CAN E-MAIL US AT:ACHARYAVISHVENDRA@GMAIL.COM

Printed by Libri Plureos GmbH in Hamburg,
Germany